CAMBRIDGE LIBRARY COLLECTION

Books of enduring scholarly value

Literary studies

This series provides a high-quality selection of early printings of literary works, textual editions, anthologies and literary criticism which are of lasting scholarly interest. Ranging from Old English to Shakespeare to early twentieth-century work from around the world, these books offer a valuable resource for scholars in reception history, textual editing, and literary studies.

Club Law

Originally written and staged in the late sixteenth century, Club Law was published for the first time more than three centuries later. A colourful satire, the play captures the spirit of a bygone era. Club Law playfully reconstructs the heated debate between the University 'Accademicks' and the town council, who were viciously at odds. Though characters' names had been changed, the play was so true to life in its depiction of contemporary politics that much uproar followed its performance at Clare Hall (now Clare College), Cambridge about 1599. Found titleless and missing some pages and scenes, the play was pieced back together by G.C. Moore Smith in 1907. A detailed introduction outlines the play's setting and historical context, and draws parallels between this satirical Elizabethan play and contemporary society. Comprehensive notes and an index are also included.

Cambridge University Press has long been a pioneer in the reissuing of out-of-print titles from its own backlist, producing digital reprints of books that are still sought after by scholars and students but could not be reprinted economically using traditional technology. The Cambridge Library Collection extends this activity to a wider range of books which are still of importance to researchers and professionals, either for the source material they contain, or as landmarks in the history of their academic discipline.

Drawing from the world-renowned collections in the Cambridge University Library, and guided by the advice of experts in each subject area, Cambridge University Press is using state-of-the-art scanning machines in its own Printing House to capture the content of each book selected for inclusion. The files are processed to give a consistently clear, crisp image, and the books finished to the high quality standard for which the Press is recognised around the world. The latest print-on-demand technology ensures that the books will remain available indefinitely, and that orders for single or multiple copies can quickly be supplied.

The Cambridge Library Collection will bring back to life books of enduring scholarly value across a wide range of disciplines in the humanities and social sciences and in science and technology.

Club Law

A Comedy

Edited by George Charles Moore Smith

CAMBRIDGE UNIVERSITY PRESS

Cambridge New York Melbourne Madrid Cape Town Singapore São Paolo Delhi

Published in the United States of America by Cambridge University Press, New York

www.cambridge.org
Information on this title: www.cambridge.org/9781108002950

This edition first published 1907
This digitally printed version 2009

ISBN 978-1-108-00295-0

CLUB LAW

CAMBRIDGE UNIVERSITY PRESS WAREHOUSE,
C. F. CLAY, MANAGER.
London: FETTER LANE, E.C.
Glasgow: 50, WELLINGTON STREET.

Leipzig: F. A. BROCKHAUS.
New York: G. P. PUTNAM'S SONS.
Bombay and Calcutta: MACMILLAN AND CO., LTD.

CLUB LAW

A COMEDY

ACTED IN CLARE HALL, CAMBRIDGE
ABOUT 1599—1600

NOW PRINTED FOR THE FIRST TIME
FROM A MS. IN THE LIBRARY OF ST JOHN'S COLLEGE
WITH AN INTRODUCTION AND NOTES

BY

G. C. MOORE SMITH, LITT.D.
PROFESSOR OF ENGLISH LANGUAGE AND LITERATURE IN THE
UNIVERSITY OF SHEFFIELD

Cambridge:
at the University Press
1907

Cambridge:
PRINTED BY JOHN CLAY, M.A.
AT THE UNIVERSITY PRESS.

PREFACE.

I TAKE this opportunity of thanking the Registrary of the University of Cambridge for giving me facilities to copy the *Acta Curiæ* and other documents preserved in the Registry: the Town Clerk of Cambridge for giving me similar facilities in regard to documents now in his charge: the Librarian and Sub-librarian of St John's College for the kind arrangements made for me in their Library: and Dr J. R. Green, Librarian of Downing College, for putting the Bowtell MSS. at my disposal at some inconvenience to himself.

I have to thank Mr J. R. Wardale and Mr H. M. Chadwick, of Clare College, for their kind readiness to help me and for their interest in my work. It is, however, a matter of regret to me that I have not had the opportunity of seeing the Bursarial Accounts of Clare College for the period in which *Club Law* was produced. Whether they contain any clue to the date of the play is very doubtful, but, at least, possible.

As my Notes show, I owe many hints and illustrations of the language of the play to the ever ready kindness and minute knowledge of my friend Mr R. B. McKerrow, the editor of Nashe, and I return him my warmest thanks.

G. C. M. S.

SHEFFIELD,
22 *June*, 1907.

TABLE OF CONTENTS.

INTRODUCTION.

I. The Manuscript of *Club Law*.

1. Fuller in his *History of the University of Cambridge* (1655) gives an amusing account of the production of a play called *Club Law* at Clare Hall in one of the last years of the 16th century. The play, we are told, which was written in English, was 'merry (but abusive),' being intended by the young scholars who composed it as a piece of revenge on the townsmen of Cambridge by whom they considered themselves wronged. Individual members of the corporation were personated to the life with their characteristic gestures and expressions, and, though many of the incidents of the play were imaginary, some came 'too near to truth' to be pleasant to the persons travestied, who had been invited to the performance and were constrained by their hosts to see it out[1].

It is not clear that Fuller had ever read the play, and I am not aware of any other reference to it in the 17th century.

In the 18th century we hear of a supposed manuscript of the play (without a title) which was in the possession of Dr Richard Farmer, Master of Emmanuel. In the Catalogue of Dr Farmer's library, issued previous to its sale in May, 1798, we have the following entries:

> '7441 The famous Tragedie of King Charles I. *imperfect*. Ditto 1649.
>
> *7441 Club-Law, a merry but abusive Comedy, MS. Acted at Clare-Hall 1597—8.'

The two items, according to two priced catalogues which I have seen, were sold together for five shillings.

[1] See the passage quoted pp. xxxix—xli.

Although rather strangely printed, I understand the word 'Ditto' to mean that the MS. of *Club Law*, like the printed Tragedy, was 'imperfect.'

This MS. of Dr Farmer's had been referred to by J. S. Hawkins in 1787 in his edition of *Ignoramus*, p. lxxii, as follows: 'Dr Farmer is in possession of a manuscript play, without a title, which from its tendency to expose the Mayor and Corporation of Cambridge, has been supposed to be *Club Law*: but as it is wholly founded on the expectation of a visit from King James, and refers to events which happened in his reign, it does not seem probable that it can be the *Club Law* which was performed in the reign of his predecessor.'

If the facts mentioned by Hawkins were correct, one might well accept his conclusion. It is clear, however, that the MS. after Dr Farmer's death was still considered to be a copy of the play mentioned by Fuller, and I am inclined to dismiss as erroneous all that Hawkins says on the Jacobean character of Dr Farmer's manuscript play.

After Dr Farmer's sale, his supposed manuscript of *Club Law* disappeared from view, and the play for more than a century was practically lost.

2. In June, 1906, when examining manuscripts of Latin academic plays in the Library of St John's College, Cambridge, I asked to see one which had been described by the late Dean Cowie in his Catalogue of the Manuscripts of the College, printed about 60 years ago, in the following terms: 'S. 62. Translation of some Latin Play (I conjecture). MS. Folio paper. The beginning is wanting.'

On examination it seemed clear that the play before me was not a translation from the Latin, but an original English play, and one that dealt with the relations of University men to the corporation of a town. For the moment I had to leave the matter there, but on reading soon afterwards Fuller's account of the play *Club Law* it occurred to me that the Cambridge manuscript was probably that comedy. In August, 1906, I transcribed the manuscript, and it became at once clear that the lost *Club Law* had come to light.

The Cambridge MS.—like that which belonged to Dr Farmer—is unfortunately imperfect. It has no title, four or five leaves are torn away at the beginning, so that we have nothing before the concluding sentence of Act I. Sc. 3, and one leaf is torn out in Act IV. containing all Sc. 3 and parts of Sc. 2 and Sc. 4 of that act. The MS. is clearly written, in a hand which may be contemporary with the play, but contains careless repetitions, omissions and distortions of words, so that in various places its interpretation presents great difficulty.

It appears—from an earlier hand-written catalogue of the MSS. of St John's College—that this MS. did not come into the possession of the College before the latter part of the 18th century. I am, therefore, inclined to think that it is the identical manuscript which belonged to Dr Farmer, and that Hawkins' account of the contents of the latter was incorrect.

It does not seem likely that St John's College purchased the MS. at Dr Farmer's sale, as otherwise the College would have probably been in possession of the printed 'Tragedie of King Charles I' which was sold with it, and this seems not to be the case. But the College may well have bought the MS. from a bookseller soon after the sale.

In the text of the play here given, the letters 's,' 'j' and 'v' have been substituted for 'ſ,' 'i' and 'u' of the MS. in accordance with modern usage, and contracted words expanded, including 'Mr' in some cases ('master'). The symbol ꝭ at the end of words, which may be read as 's' or 'es,' has been printed 's' (*e.g.* 'vassalls,' 'lodgings,' 'maks,' 'magistrats,' 'thats,' 'letts'), except in the case of 'priviledges' (l. 2776), where it makes a syllable. All words inserted in the text have been enclosed in square brackets, and all words omitted or altered have been mentioned in footnotes.

All deviations from the punctuation of the MS. have been mentioned in a list appended to the text.

II. Town and Gown at Cambridge at the end of the 16th Century.

1. Our play *Club Law* owed its origin to a long-standing feud between the University and the town of Cambridge, which at the close of the 16th century had become specially acute. Before we can place it, we must therefore understand the circumstances out of which it arose. The ground of the quarrels which so often occurred between the two bodies was the possession by the University of extraordinary privileges which had descended to it from the Middle Ages.

The first of such privileges was the power to regulate the supply and price of provisions in Cambridge by exercising its own jurisdiction over 'Regraters, Forestallers and Ingrossers[1].' This power was derived from a charter granted to the University by Henry III (22nd February, 126$\frac{7}{8}$)[2], of which the third article ran as follows: 'quod nullus Regratarius emat victualia in villa Cantabrig. vel extra versus villam venientia, nec aliquid emat vt iterum vendat ante horam tertiam, et si fecerit, amercietur secundum quantitatem et qualitatem delicti.'

By a charter of King Edward II dated 14th February, 131$\frac{6}{7}$, previous grants to the University were confirmed, and the following privilege added. We quote Cooper's translation[3]:

'VII. That whenever the mayor and bailiffs should take their oath of fealty in their Common Hall, the Corporation should forewarn the Chancellor of the day in order that he (by himself or by some other person) might be present if he would, (which oath as far as regards the scholars should be that they, the said mayor and bailiffs will maintain to the best of their power

[1] Strictly, a 'regrater' was one who bought to sell again, a 'forestaller' one who bought goods before they came into the market, an 'ingrosser' one who bought up goods with the view of getting practically a monopoly. But the terms are often used with little distinction of meaning.

[2] Cooper's *Annals*, I. 50.

[3] Cooper, I. 75.

the liberties and customs of the University as concerning the keeping of the King's peace and the assise of bread and beer and other victuals, and that they will not wilfully or maliciously impugn the other liberties and lawful customs of the University) and that otherwise the oath of fealty should be of no avail: but if the Chancellor after being forewarned would not be present by himself or his Proctor, the said oath should nevertheless be taken.'

This provision was confirmed by charter of King Edward III dated 20th March, 133$\frac{5}{6}$[1].

A new charter, still more comprehensive and explicit, was granted by Richard II, 17th February, 138$\frac{1}{2}$[2].

This provided that the University authorities should have 'the custody of the assize of bread wine and beer and the punishment of the same[3]', and should 'have power to inquire and take conusance of forestallers and regrators, and of putrid...flesh and fish, in the town and suburbs, and to make due punishment thereupon.'

A further charter, granted by the same King on 10th December, 1383[4], provided that the Chancellor for the time being and his vice-gerent 'should for ever have before their conusance of all and all manner of personal pleas as well of debts, accounts and all other contracts and injuries, as of trespasses against the peace and misprisions whatsoever done within the town of Cambridge or the suburbs (mayhem[5] and felony only excepted) where a Master, scholar or scholar's servant or a common minister of the University should be a party.' (Hence arose the troublesome class of 'privileged persons' against whom action in most cases could only be taken in the Vice-Chancellor's court.) 'That no justice, judge, sheriff, mayor, bailiff or any other minister, should interfere in the pleas aforesaid, or put any party to answer before them, unless

[1] Cooper, I. 88.   [2] Cooper, I. 124.

[3] *i.e.* the power of fixing by proclamation from time to time the price at which bread, wine and beer should be sold, and of punishing those who demanded more than the price permitted.

[4] Cooper, I. 127.

[5] 'Mayhem' (or 'maim') means an injury causing privation of some essential part.

the Chancellor or his vice-gerent should be found defective in administering justice....' 'That the Chancellor and his successors or their vice-gerents might imprison all persons convicted before them in the Castle of Cambridge, or elsewhere in the town, at their discretion.'

Under 1386 Cooper tells us[1] that the Chancellor claimed to have the correction and punishment of those who sold candles and fuel, under the grant conferring on him the government of victuals, and the King declared by letters patent that chandlers and hostellers should in future be reputed victuallers and should be subject to the Chancellor's correction.

In consequence of frequent disputes between the town and University both parties in 1502 besought the amicable interference of Margaret, Countess of Richmond and Derby, the King's mother. She advised them to appoint arbitrators to determine their respective claims. The award—made under their seals and the seal of the Countess—was, in 1503, reduced to the form of an indenture of covenant between the two corporations[2]. But Cooper adds 'the disputes between the two bodies were renewed, even during the life of the Countess of Richmond.'

The privileges of the University were confirmed by a new charter granted by Queen Elizabeth, 26th April, 1561[3], one clause of which provided that the authorities of the University 'as well by day as by night, at their pleasure, might make scrutiny, search, and inquisition, in the town and suburbs, and in Barnwell and Sturbridge, for all common women, bawds, vagabonds, and other suspected persons...and punish all whom on such scrutiny, search, and inquisition, they should find guilty or suspected of evil, by imprisonment of their bodies, banishment, or otherwise as the Chancellor or his vice-gerent should deem fit.' The Mayor and other officers of the town were commanded not to impede such search, but on request of the Chancellor or his vice-gerent to aid and assist therein.

[1] Cooper, I. 131.
[2] Cooper, I. 258, 260, etc.
[3] Cooper, II. 165—168.

The privileges given by the various royal charters were confirmed to the University by Act of Parliament in 1571[1].

Under these charters the University had great powers of interference with the trade of the town and of entrance into the houses of the townsmen: it could summon offenders before its own courts and commit them to prison, whereas members of the University and their servants could not be brought before the courts of the town except for the sole crimes of mayhem and felony: it had the further right of exacting an oath from every incoming Mayor of Cambridge that he would preserve the University's privileges.

2. Every occasion was thus given for disputes between the two bodies. The townsmen—feeling themselves not to be masters in their own house—were apt to rebel against the restrictions laid on them: and members of the University were equally ready to resent the least infringement of the rights they had enjoyed for so many centuries.

We need not go back to an earlier point than the year 1586—7, a year marked by events which anticipated those of 1596 and the years following with which we are more immediately concerned.

The Mayor, John Edmunds—although the son of a previous Vice-Chancellor—on his entering on office at Michaelmas, 1586, contrived that scarcely anyone should be present when he took the oath to the University except himself and the Town Clerk. Six months later the Mayor impounded some hogs belonging to one Hammond, bailiff and brewer of Jesus College: and in consequence on 27th May, 1587, the Vice-Chancellor and the major part of the Heads of Colleges and other Doctors then in the University, made a decree prohibiting, under a penalty of 100 shillings, any scholar or person having scholar's privilege to buy, sell, contract or communicate with the Mayor on account

[1] Cooper, II. 274.

of his ingratitude to the University. Such a decree was and is called one of 'discommoning[1].'

Meanwhile, the Vice-Chancellor having arrested two persons for impounding the hogs, and having kept one in prison, had been served at the Mayor's instigation in a very offensive manner with two writs of *habeas corpus* to remove the delinquents and their causes to the Court of Queen's Bench.

It was alleged by the Mayor that the pound had been twice sawn asunder by multitudes of riotous persons with clubs and the hogs delivered, and that the rioters threatened with clubs to beat into their doors all such persons as came out to see who they were[2].

[1] After the discommoning the following Grace was submitted (British Museum Additional MSS. 5852, fo. 82, etc.—Cole's copy of a MS. lent him by Dr Farmer):

'Junii 12, 1587. Oppidani suspensi in gratiam non nisi a senatu recipiendi.

'Cum superioribus hisce Diebus quidam Oppidani propter Demerita sua et intollerabilem adversus Academiam et Academicos Ingratitudinem a Contubernio Scholarium sunt suspensi, et Scholares et eorum Famuli cum eisdem quovis modo contrahere aut negotiari stricte et sub gravi mulcta sunt interdicti, Placet vobis ut hujusmodi antedicta Decreta et in inposterum decernenda vestra auctoritate rata et firma teneantur et inposterum non rescindantur sine consensu et assensu totius Senatus, etc.'

The University based its right to 'discommon' on its possession of ecclesiastical jurisdiction. Cp. a passage in 'A Projecte conteyninge the state, order, and manner of Governemente of the University of Cambridge' [in 1601], printed by Cooper (*Annals*, II. 602—611):

(p. 609) 'The University is authorized to use or exercise jurisdiction ecclesiastical, as appeareth by the grant of King Richard the Second, in the 7th yeare of his raigne, and by his writts of prohibition...sent to the Courte of the Arches, and...to the Official, or Commissary unto John Bishop of Ely...prohibiting those Courtes from the sending forth of any inhibitions or citations to the Chanceller of the University of Cambridge; which is also confirmed by the continual practice of the University ever since the said time, as may be shewed by the probate of the Wills or Testaments of priviledged persons dyinge within that Body: *By the excommunicating of divers Maiors of the Towne of Cambridge for impugning the knowne priviledges of the University, contrary to their othe*; and by the ordinary censuringe of Incontinencye...the party there offending being of the priviledge of the University.'

[2] Cooper, II. 437—441. MS. in Registry, 37. 2. 62.

On 4th September Henry Clarke, an Alderman, was also discommoned for having withdrawn his custom from Hammond, and John Jenkynson, late bailiff of the town, for having tried to dissuade others from dealing with Hammond. Alderman Clarke subsequently submitted himself and was forgiven.

On 5th July all persons enjoying University privileges were forbidden to sell or give to the town lands or houses belonging to the University or Colleges—this being done in retaliation for an ordinance of the Corporation prohibiting the transference of property of that body to others than burgesses, and on 13th October a Grace was passed that all privileged persons who had taken the oath to the University and had afterwards become members of the Corporation of the town should be *ipso facto* separated from communion with the scholars for ever[1].

In 1589, after many years of fruitless negotiation, the University and the town came to an agreement as to the terms of their respective charters in regard to Sturbridge Fair. But the concordat did not give complete satisfaction to the townspeople, and the Mayor, Nicholas Gaunt, who had assented to the University's charter, was considered to have betrayed the town. In consequence he was 'shortlie after putt of his Aldermanshipp and lived the remaynder of his life in great want and miserie and hatefull to all the townesmen[2].'

In $15\frac{89}{90}$ letters were received by Mayors of towns from the Privy Council concerning the killing of flesh in Lent, and the Mayor of Cambridge took upon him to take bond for the due observing of the order from certain butchers and victuallers. As the University claimed that any such proceeding was entirely in its own province, it sent a protest to Lord Burghley. It complained especially against Lord North (Lord Lieutenant of the county and High Steward of the town) for supporting the town in thus infringing University privileges[3].

In September, 1591, one Richard Parish of Chesterton attacked

[1] Cooper, II. 448. [2] Cooper, II. 466—475.
[3] Cooper, II. 481—483.

and wounded some scholars. A complaint having been made, the Vice-Chancellor issued a decree for the man's arrest, which was executed as he was in attendance on Lord North and other justices returning from the sessions. He was rescued by Lord North's retinue, but 'the scholars raised the cry of clubs which was promptly responded to and an affray took place in which Lord North appears to have been placed in some little peril.' He preferred a complaint to the Privy Council. The matter was investigated by the Privy Council on 23rd November, but it does not appear how it ended[1].

About the year 1596 the townsmen drew up articles of complaint against the University. In these were recited various acts of oppression committed within 15 or 20 years preceding, generally by the Taxors or Proctors in the exercise of their right to enter houses in search of criminals or loose women or to stop the conveyance out of Cambridge of candles or corn or the selling of wine without a licence. They also included charges against the University officials of accepting money for permission to do things otherwise forbidden. Article 31 runs as follows: 'They have brought back againe with force divers vessells laden with corne of sondrie persons lawfullie licenced by the Justices, mysseusinge the Corne with wetinge yt and dasshinge yt, and thrustinge a greate deale thereof into the River, and without money will not suffer it to passe[2].' We shall find a similar occurrence in our play.

This year the University took great offence at the issuing of a commission of the peace in which the name of the Mayor, who was appointed *Custos Rotulorum*, was placed before that of the Vice-Chancellor[3].

The Mayor elected at Michaelmas of this year, Robert Wallis, refused to take the oath for the conservation of the University's privileges. Complaint having been made, the matter was referred on the part of the two Corporations to Lord Keeper Egerton as

[1] Cooper, II. 493—508. [2] Cooper, II. 548—556.
[3] Cooper, II. 557.

Recorder of the town and Lord Burghley as Chancellor of the University, who made an order on 12th November directing that notice should be given to the Vice-Chancellor two days before the Mayor and bailiffs took the oath of fidelity and that the oath should thereafter be taken in the presence of the Vice-Chancellor[1].

On the 13th December at a meeting of the two bodies in St Mary's the Mayor again refused to take the oath, alleging that the order made was prospective only and charging Lord Burghley with overruling the matter against all law and right. On which the University again complained to the Chancellor[2].

[1] Camb. Univ. MSS. Mm. I. 35. 2.

'November 12. 1596

'The ordre for the Mayors oath.

'Whereas by the Charter graunted to the Universitie by Kinge Edward the second, & divers tymes since confirmed, It doth appeare that the Comminalty of the Towne of Cambr: should premonere Cancellarium vel per se vel per certas aliquas personas, intersit prestationi Juramenti fidelitatis Majoris et Ballivorum as by the sd. Charter more at large appeareth. And whereas the Vicechan: of the Universitie for the tyme being hath been accustomed by himselfe or such as he hath assigned, to minister an oath to the sd Mayor & Bayliffs for the tyme being, according to the sd Charter, viz: quod ipsi Major et Ballivi libertates et consuetudines universitatis predicte quoad conservationem pacis nostre et assise panis et cervisie ac victualium pro viribus conservabunt et quod alias libertates et consuetud: eiusdem Universitatis debitas, quatenus sibi de eisdem constiterit indebite seu malitiose non impugnabunt. And yet notwithstandinge of late the Mayor & Bayliffs of Cambr. have moved some question, as well concerning the sd premonition, as also concerninge the ministring of ye sd. oath, we therefore the L. Keeper of the great Seale of Englande now Recorder of ye Towne of Cambr, & the L High Tre—r of England, being the Chancellour of the Universitie of Cambr: respecting the good and quiet both of ye Universitie & Towne...do ordre and determine, that from hence forth premonition shall be given to the Vicechan: or his Deputie for the tyme beinge, by the Comminalty of the Towne of Cambr: two dayes before the Mayor and Bayliffs shall take y^r^ oath of fidelity: and that the Mayor & Bayliffs for the tyme being, & all y^r^ successors shall for ever herafter take the sd oath (accordinge to the sd. Charter as is before expressed) beinge reade by the Proctors of the Universitie or y^r^ Deputies, as heretofore hath bene accustomed, in the presence of the Vice Chan: for the tyme beinge; or in the presence of two Doctors, or two Heades of Colledges in the sd. Universitie, to be specially in y^r^ behalfe appoynted.

....

Tho: Egerton C.S. W. Burghley.'

[2] Cooper, II. 558.

Meanwhile on the 13th November the townsmen send to the Lord Keeper and Lord Burghley fresh articles against the University. Among other things they complain of discommoning, they say the Court of the Consistory of the University is rightly called by the University-men the townsmen's scourge and they make a statement of ill-usage suffered by the Mayor, to which we shall have occasion to refer later[1].

On the 19th January Dr Jegon the Vice-Chancellor complained to Archbishop Whitgift that the Mayor and his brethren had taken occasion of the receipt of letters from the Privy Council concerning the assising of the price of grain in markets and the correction of victuallers, to interfere in matters which were the prerogative of the University[2].

On the preceding 28th September two maltsters named Nicholson and Rose had been fined in the University leet for ingrossing corn. We shall hear more of this case later[3].

At the town sessions held on 24th May, 1597, a dispute took place between Dr Jegon, the Vice-Chancellor, and the Mayor and other Justices with regard to the jurisdiction of the University over townsmen accused of forestalling and ingrossing and its sole jurisdiction over its own members and 'privileged persons.' In consequence the townsmen preferred a complaint to Lord Burghley the Chancellor, and the Vice-Chancellor submitted a reply to it on 23rd June.

In his letter to Lord Burghley enclosing the reply, Dr Jegon speaks of 'the quarrelous disposition and insolent behavior of our neighbours of the Towne, beinge (as is observed by the ancyentest and gravest amongst us) more factious and stirringe now of late then in former tymes, making choise of suche to be governoures amongest them, as are most boulde and forward in attemptes against this University.' On the same day the Vice-Chancellor and the Heads officially frame a complaint against 'the mayor and townsmen of Cambridge': 'They summon our

[1] Cooper, II. 559—561. [2] Cooper, II. 565.
[3] Cooper, II. 566, 567.

known privileged persons to their town sessions; they award process against them; they daily commit them; they openly discharge victuallers; they take scholars' horses to serve post upon ordinary commission; and generally they adventure to do any thing against our charters with such unwonted boldness and violence, that we shall be driven of necessity to seek relief extraordinary.'

Some of the townsmen having on their part complained to Lord Chief Justice Popham of high-handed and irregular proceedings on the part of the University, he wrote a severe letter to the Vice-Chancellor on 4th July. It was one element in the situation that in resisting the privileges conferred on the University by charter the townsmen generally had the sympathy of those who administered the common law of the land[1]. Lord Burghley also advised the Vice-Chancellor to 'carry himself in temperate sorte towards the mayor and his company.' In return however the Vice-Chancellor on 26th July sent to Lord Burghley a series of 'articles of grievances done by Mr Maior of Cambridge against the Universitie.' The last article is of special interest to us.

'11. Hughe Jones, sometimes servaunt to the Taxer of the Universitie, discharged that Universitie service, and banished that bodie for his corrupt dealinge and other misdemeanour in his service, att the suite and petition of Mr Clarke Alderman, is now by this Maior preferred to be Sergeant unto the towne, being a man manie wayes infamous, as being a fitt instrument to deale (as he notoriouslie doth) against the Universitie.'

In a new complaint against the Mayor and townsmen made

[1] Thus the solicitor for the University, Mr Philip Stringer, writes to Dr Jegon from London on 3rd November, 1597:

'My Lord Cheife Justice...is peremptorie in this, that our Charter doth not give us cognisance of any thinge w[ch] is not triable at the Common Lawe of England, or that it can be an offence in Cambridge betwixt subjecte & subjecte & there punishable, eyther by lawe or custome, w[ch] is not an offence & so unpunishable in other partes of the Lande: & must therefore be (as he sayth) a meere usurpac'on & not a right use of our Charter.' (Baker MSS.)

to Lord Burghley on 27th September the following article perhaps refers to the same action:

'3. Notoriouse lewde persons by consent of the Vice-Chancellor and heades thrust out from serving the Universitie officers, for abusinge some cheife men of the towne, and for corrupt dealinge under their maisters, are made officers and free burgesses of their bodie, to nourishe (as we suppose) occasion of dislike and contention betwene us.'

Another clause runs as follows:

'Lastlie whereas we have received diverse lettres from...hir Majesties privie Counsell for reformation of Ingrossers of Corne, and thereupon have bine very carefull to enquire and amercie in our Leete or Laweday such offenders accordinge to our Charter and auncient Custome, the Townesmen (offendors in that behalf) are so farr from reforminge themselves, as that not onlie they doe soe still: but alsoe take exceptiones against our proceedinges, Threateninge Indictmentes of premunire &c.[1]'

Robert Wallis was re-elected Mayor for 1597—8 and took his oath on Michaelmas Day for the conservation of University privileges but in an irreverent manner, keeping his head covered. Fresh complaints to Lord Burghley followed[2].

Dr Jegon, who was re-elected Vice-Chancellor, having committed to prison William Nicholson for refusing to pay his debt to the Proctors and three other persons for other reasons, writs of *habeas corpus* were sued out of the Court of King's Bench, and on the last day of Michaelmas term the Court adjudged the Vice-Chancellor's returns bad, and in spite of his humble submission by the mouth of his counsel amerced him in £20 for his returns and in a further sum of £20 for the false imprisonment of the parties[3].

This was a triumph for the town, as we see from a letter written by the Vice-Chancellor and Heads to Lord Chief Justice Popham apparently on 1st January, 159$\frac{7}{8}$, 'our Adversaries so greatly triumphe in that displeasure which (they give out) they

[1] Cooper, II. 572—579. [2] Cooper, II. 582.
[3] Cooper, II. 585.

have wrought us with your Lordship, that the meanest people here (by their Encouragement) doe beginne to resist us in all our courses of goverment.' They protest against having to plead their charters in court and ask that the Lord Chief Justice would hear their cause in private.

Their position was more clearly expressed in a letter to Lord Burghley of 15th March, in which they write: 'the wordes of our Charter, as we take it, doe utterly free us from those Courtes, neither are we to aunswere our proceedinges before any Judge or Justice but yourselfe our Chancellour (except for maheme and fellonie)[1].'

From a letter of Dr Jegon's of 8th May it would seem that he thought that he had satisfied the Court of King's Bench of the validity of his proceedings against Nicholson and the others who had sued out writs of *habeas corpus*[2]. The result however seems to show that he was under some error.

Lord Burghley having died on 4th August, the University on the 10th elected the Earl of Essex to the Chancellorship, and during the following months made efforts to enlist him actively in its cause. He satisfied it in one respect, as the following shows:

'I do set down this judgment as earl marshall of England and judge by my office of all places and precedencies that the vice chancellor of Cambridge is to be in commission before the mayor.

'ESSEX[3].'

Soon after Lord Essex became Chancellor he visited Cambridge. The Attorney General Coke seems to have been there at the same time and to have allowed himself to be convinced of the justice of the University's pretensions[4].

About this time the University again formulated complaints

[1] Cooper, II. 589, 590.

[2] Cooper, II. 590, 591.

[3] Cooper, II. 594.

[4] Letter of Dr Jegon and the Heads to Lord Essex, 28th October, 1598: 'our knowne priviledges, (so deemed vppon a deliberate Hearinge in y^r owne presence by Mr Atturney General).' (Baker MSS. xxiv. 378.)

against the town and Robert Wallis the Mayor. Those against Wallis were as follows:

'1. who set at libertie Jo. Tiddiswell, Geor. Pretty and Edw. Hurste—being in execucion upon the Vicechancellours sentence.

'2. who imprisoned Jo. Longworth the late Proctors man for misdemeanoure in his behaviour towards the said Wallis.

'3. who called together a company of his owne spirit and faction for ye disfranchisinge of the burgesses aboue mencioned [*sc.* in the earlier part of the complaints] & did effect it accordingly.

'4. who hath attempted in open sessions with ye assistance of Mr Francis Brakin their deputie Recorder and a towne-borne man to infringe ye knowne priviledges of the universitie by summoning of victuallers thether.

'5. who beinge app^d^. a commissioner for the subsidie did purposely forbeare to appointe any scholler &c to haue the truste of a sessor.

'6. and lastly who not longe since in thende of his Maioralty hath most ambitiously procured himselfe and one Jo: Yaxley a yonge Bencher[1] as they call him, and a man of his owne humor and discretion to be put into the commission of ye peace, y^t^ so howsoeuer any other of the Towne stand affected, they may still take occasion to disturbe the quiet of that place; and to hinder any thinge well intended there as was very apparent in the first Sessions after thei were placed in y^t^ commission, at which meetinge ye said Yaxley most insolently affirmed y^t^ vpon his owne knowledge he durst undertake to say y^t^ it was intended by ye last Statute de anno 39 Eliz concerning the releife of ye pore that none should haue to doe therein but the Mayor of the Towne[2], and y^t^ he would not for his owne parte be ordered by any other notwithstanding yt the whole company (except his fellowe Wallis) thought otherwise of it[3].'

[1] That is, Alderman. Cp. Cooper, III. 47 'the bench and the form.'

[2] Yaxley with Wallis had represented Cambridge in the Parliament summoned on the 24th October, 1597, and dissolved on the 9th February, 159$\frac{7}{8}$.

[3] 'Letters...in the tyme of Dr Jegon' in the University Registry.

The last clause introduces us to a character who was perhaps a more violent opponent of the University than Wallis had been.

James Robson was elected Mayor for 1598—9 and Dr Jegon re-elected Vice-Chancellor. From the following document[1], which is probably to be dated December, 1598, we see the anxiety of the University to have Wallis and Yaxley removed from the Commission of the Peace.

'Directions for the renuinge of the Commission of the Peace for the Universitie & Towne of Cambridge.

'First that my L. the Earle of Essex be placed in the Commission...who was not in the last Commission procured in June last by Wallys and Yaxley.

'...That special suite be made with the privity of our Ho: Chan: & by his Lps direction for the removinge of Wallis & Yaxley out of the commission, for that they were put into it by y^r^ owne ambitions, seeking thereof to disquiet the goverment of the universitie & of the Towne also, as we have found to our great charge, & would be found also by the best sorte of the Towne, if they were therin examined: both the Universitie & Towne having cause so to thinke, by such conference as the goverment of those Bodyes have had for the good of the Towne since Wallys left to be Mayor there; & are of opinion, that if it should be thought meete to have more of the Townsmen in Commission, that other amongst them might be found farr meeter for that purpose then eyther Wallys or Yaxley, as namely the Mayor for the tyme beinge whose name is James Robson, & one Mr Medcalfe, who hath bene mayor long since, who are knowne to be men of quieter spirits, & every waye more meete then the other for that service.'

In Trinity term, 1599, judgment was given in the Court of Common Pleas in an action for assault and false imprisonment on 23rd September, 1597, brought by William Nicholson, maltster,

[1] Cambridge University Library, MS. Mm. 1. 35 (xxx) fo. 386.

against the late Vice-Chancellor, Dr Jegon, and Benjamin Pryme, the inferior bedell of the University.

'The defendants...alleged that the University was a Corporation by prescription, and had a Court of Record at which the inhabitants ought to enquire of forestallers, regrators and engrossers,...and that they had a right to imprison on non-payment of fines and forfeitures imposed in such Court. They then set out the Queen's charter of 26th April 1561 and the confirmation thereof by parliament, and averred that on 1st Augt. 1596 the plaintiff engrossed three quarters of barley, buying it out of the market of divers persons with intent to sell it again, and that at the Leet held on 28th Sept. following, before Lionel Duckett and Thomas Cooke, proctors, the plaintiff was fined 20*s*. for that offence, and refusing to pay was imprisoned. To this plea the plaintiff demurred, and the Court gave judgment in his favour.' The damages were assessed at £40 and the costs taxed at £7[1].

In a paper in the Record Office[2] called 'A breife of articles [against the town] answeres [by the town] and replies [by the University] examined at Lambeth A° dni 1599 Eliz. 41. (*i.e.* before November 20th),' one grievance of the University is summarised 'Resistance of search by Wallis and Slegge' (Slegge was the Town Clerk). This was justified by the town '1° because no tippling howse, 2° because no suspected persons,' to which the University replied by a reference to the Act of Parliament of 1561 which gave the Chancellor a right of search 'per se per suos etc quandocunque atque ubicunque infra villam etc visum fuerit.'

In the autumn of this year John Yaxley became Mayor for 1599—1600, and Dr Soame of Peterhouse Vice-Chancellor. We have a fairly complete list of the Mayor, Aldermen and 'Four and Twenty' or 'Brethren' at this time as we find that on the 4th December, 1599, John Yaxley, Mayor, John Edmonds, William Wulfe, Thomas Metcalfe, Robert Wallis, John Norkot, James

[1] Cooper, II. 596.

[2] *State Papers*, Domestic Series, Elizabeth, vol. 273.

Robson, Jeremy Chace, John Jenkinson, William Nicholson, and Edward Potto, Aldermen, chose the following into the number of the Four and Twenty:

John Tiddeswell,	Miles Goldsborow,	John Andrewes,
Thomas Manninge,	Richard Bembridge,	Hugh Rose,
Thomas Emons,	John Hawkins,	Godfrey Twelves,
Richard Jones,	John Fidlinge,	William Archer,
John Holmes,	John Haselopp,	John Dawson,
William Andrewes,	Thomas Tomson,	John Wickstedd,
Martyn Wharton,	Thomas Smart,	John Durant,
John Goodwyn,	Peter Whaley,	Thomas Frenche[1].

Yaxley as Mayor seems to have made himself very obnoxious to the University.

A contemporary writes[2]:

'1600. This year first were most of our Boddy cessed by the meanes of Mr Yaxley, being Maior, at Lands, for the Subsidy, hoping therby to make us Contributors. This year did the same man Mr Yaxley proclame hymself sole Governer in Sturbrydg Fayre, & tooke away the Scalles one Honny Hill [in the fair], wich afterward he was glad to set them[3] agayne[4].'

And a year later Chief Justice Popham, writing to the then Mayor of Cambridge, Mr Chase, on the subject of a joint contribution from the Town and University to the poor of three parishes[5], remarks:

'I did well like that the Towne & Vniversitie did ioyne togither in these...services. But must needes myslyke with the course held by your predecessour Mr Yaxley who did impugne a good & neccessarie ordre continued afore by his predecessours for the relefe of the poore and am very sory that you will followe his pre-

[1] Cooper, II. 597 (from Metcalfe MS. in Downing Coll.).

[2] British Museum Add. MSS. 5852, fo. 89 (a transcript by Cole of papers lent him by Dr Farmer).

[3] ? 'there.'

[4] See the Queen's letter of 27th August, 1601 (Cooper, II. 612).

[5] Cp. Cooper, II. 594 top.

sident....M[r] Yaxley did other wise then was warrantable by lawe & withall is suspected to haue bene a meane to nourish vnkindenes betwene the Towne & the Vniversitie which for my owne parte I would be glad to be at vnitie that the publique service be not, be the crosse humours of some, neglected.

'Bury, 3 Ap. 1601[1].'

The *Acta Curiæ* of the University show that on one occasion at least the hostile feeling provoked by Mr Yaxley as Mayor took an overt form. On the 14th December George Bubworth, brewer, and two of his servants was sued 'for certaine misdemeanours and outerages by them done last nighte, especially against Mr Maior of Cambridge.' The Vice-Chancellor committed Bubworth to the Tolbooth to remain there during his good pleasure. However, on 11th January the Mayor signified to the Vice-Chancellor that Bubworth had been with him that morning and had made his submission, and that he was now satisfied; and on the 25th the Vice-Chancellor, after enjoining Bubworth to pay 6*s*. 8*d*. for the use of the poor of St Michael's parish (in which Mr Yaxley lived), and seeing the money paid, terminated the proceedings.

In the autumn of 1600 Mr Yaxley was succeeded in the mayoralty by Mr Jeremy Chace and Dr Soame by Dr Jegon, who was now Vice-Chancellor for the fourth time.

Things had not improved during the year of his interregnum. Within a few days of his entering on office he writes that Bedell Pryme has been imprisoned 'per grassantem oppidanorum injuriam': complains of 'the greate insolencie of our Townesmen,' and says, 'They now adventure to break our Charters in all thynges and proclayme themselves sole governors in this place, whereupon execucion of Justice, releefe of y[e] poore and all good discipline is so much neglected that I fearfully forethinke what is likely to followe, the multitudes of both bodies being so much intemperate[2].'

On 10th February, 160$\frac{0}{1}$, a statement of grievances was sent to

[1] 'Copies of diverse letters...' vol. II., in the University Registry.

[2] Letters of Dr Jegon of 7th, 8th and 19th November, 1600, in the University Registry.

Sir Robert Cecil and other persons of influence. It was in these terms:

'1. Subsidiorum imposicionibus inauditis onerant quos munificentissima princeps semper et ubique liberos esse voluit.

'2. Scholares cuiusque ordinis procancellarium ipsum indebite ad forinseca tribunalia trahunt [&] acerrime persequuntur.

'3. Pupillos nostros ad clandestinos contractus et dispar conjugium in ædibus suis pelliciunt nec officiarios nostros per solitum scrutinium ibidem investigare sinunt.

'4. Servos nostros ante lares, ad ipsas collegiorum portas adoriuntur, gladiis vulnerant.

'5. Juramentum pro conservacione pacis perpetuis temporibus elapsis admissum omnino respuunt.

'6. Maiorem suum quem vocant unicum huius municipii magistratum esse publico præconio clamitant[1].'

On the 14th February, 160$\frac{0}{1}$, on the eve of Lord Essex's conviction for high treason, Sir Robert Cecil was elected Chancellor of the University. In a paper dated 14th July following, in which he requests some gentlemen resident near Cambridge to investigate the matters in dispute between the Town and the University, he writes: 'I must confess it greeves me not a litle to finde so greate opposition between the two Bodies...for first that excellent nursery of Learning is dayly vexed with matter of contention and quarrell from the Town....Secondly the Town...like to be impoverished by maintaining of suites.' In some particulars he admits that he has found 'over sights on the part of some... rash-headed Schollers in the University,' but he says that, in the efforts he has made for peace, he has seen that the Town 'sought to raise new doubts even so far as tended to the prejudice and annihilating of the...Charter' (which the Queen would not hear of)[2].

Drs Jegon, Goade, and Tyndall at this time sent some suggestions to the Chancellor for settling the disputes. In them

[1] Letters...in the University Registry.

[2] *State Papers*, Domestic Series, Elizabeth, vol. 281 (14).

we see some indications that the proceedings of the University were felt to have been open to some exception. The suggestions are thus summarised in the *Calendar of State Papers*[1]:

'1. Alehouses—if the number be found excessive, to endeavour to suppress the over number.

'2. For the mittimus we are ready to yield, in case of execution, to any course according to the proceedings of civil law.

'3. For avoiding abuses in nightly searches by young deputy proctors, we agree to order that none be appointed deputy proctors in that case but masters of arts of three years standing, and such as the Vicechancellor shall allow: and for avoiding counterfeit proctors, they shall carry in all searches the proctor's staff, being the ensign appointed for that purpose.

'4. We are willing to effect a meet contribution to the poor either to the use of the inhabitants of the town, if the townsmen will accept it as of free benevolence and not as compelled by law, or else to relieve the poor of our own body, and the town the poor of theirs.

'5. That the officers of the University shall not hold plea of any penal law but such as concern victuals and victuallers, forestallers and regrators, and such as are granted to them by the laws and statutes of the realm.'

This document is accompanied by a 'Petition for orders to prevent future disquiet,' of which the purport is as follows:

'1. Order in complaining—That they break not the order of the Lady Margaret's composition.

'2. Penalty for not proving. That when they shall complain...and thereby draw privileged persons to charge and fail in proofs, then they shall bear the charges of the defendants molested....

'3. That we maye have o^r^ wonted neighborlie meetinge by publique & mutuall conferrence to compounde grevaunces in

[1] *State Papers*, Domestic Series, Elizabeth, vol. 281 (15, 16).

tyme, wch meetinges (tendered by vs vnto them) have bene of late yeares by ye insolente frowardnes of Mr Wallis maior for two yeares together & Mr Yaxly for one yeare broken of and discontinued.

'5. ...we wishe a speedy renewinge of the Co͞mission. In wch Co͞mission yf Mr Wallis and Mr Yaxly the cheife disturbers of co͞mon quiet were lefte out,...it would be a meanes expediente & effectuall for the quiet of both Bodyes.

'John Jegon vican:

'Roger Goad

'Humph. Tyndall.'

Robert Wallis and John Yaxley represented Cambridge in the two last Parliaments of Queen Elizabeth (24th October, 1597—9th February, 159$\frac{7}{8}$, and 27th October, 1601—19th December, 1601) and in the first Parliament of James I (19th March, 160$\frac{3}{4}$—9th February, 16$\frac{10}{11}$).

Appendix.

It may be interesting to append to the above history a paper of unknown authorship dating from the latter half of the 18th century[1] and showing the view taken by a townsman of University privileges at that date. The paper is preserved in the office of the Town Clerk of Cambridge, who kindly allowed me to copy it.

'It is a fact that formerly the Mayor and Corporation, attended by two inhabitants of each parish in the town, were required by the Univ^{y} to meet the V.C. in the vestry room of S. Mary the Great on the first sunday after his initiation into office, there to be sworn by or before him to be at all times ready to aid and assist him and the other officers of the Univ^{y} in preserving the peace and good order of the town and univ^{y}. Nearly two centuries past a gentleman, who was Mayor of the Corporation, did

[1] The reference to the suspension of Habeas Corpus (see p. xxxiv) suggests that the date was either 1777—9 or 1794, but I know nothing of any aggressive action of a Vice-Chancellor at either of these dates. If by the Mayor of 'nearly two centuries ago' Edmunds is meant (see p. xv), the date must be the earlier one.

refuse to perform this act of humiliation and for this he and the whole corporation were discommuned. By the act, statute, or decree of discommuning every member of the Univ^{y} is forbidden under the pains and penalties of heavy fine and expulsion from the Univ^{y} to have any sort of dealing with any one so discommuned. This discommuning continued some weeks, when so considerable was the injury sustained by the members of the corporation, that the Mayor was intreated and induced to offer a most humble and earnest petition to the V. C. praying that the corporation might be re-admitted to favour, and promising never more to offend in the premises. On this the discommuning was taken of, and the amende honorable was made in the vestry of St Mary's Church. This homage it seems has been discontinued for a very long period. The present V. C. demands the renewal of it, and holding as he does the keys of the Univ^{y} treasury in his hands he refuses to pay to the Overseers of the poor the dues or allowances, which the Univ^{y} have been accustomed from time immemorial to pay them towards the maintenance of the poor of the town. This is the pretext, which the V. C. sets forth, but that it has nothing to do with the case must it is presumed be clear to every one. The parochial dues or allowances referred to are either a free-gift of the University, or a composition in lieu of poor rates. If the former we have nothing to say to it only that it is a disgrace to the inhabitants of the town of Cambridge to accept alms in any form or from any body of men whatever. If the latter (a compromise in lieu of poor rates) then it bears no proportion at all to the sum due and owing by the Univ^{y} to the town.

'It is, doubtless, very true that in their first institution most of our colleges were eleemosynary foundations. They were founded long before the poor laws were in existence, at the time when the necessitous poor were almost entirely supported by the contributions of ecclesiastick and monastick incorporations. They (the colleges) were neither subject to tonnage, poundage, tenths, fifteenths or other taxes to the state. They were a sort of alms-houses, into which idle necessitous and cunning people for the most part obtained admittance or were placed to learn the art of supporting by an appearance of piety and science the popular and reigning superstitions and impositions of the age. But "Tempora mutantur et nos mutamur in illis." The Univ[y] along with everything else has undergone a complete change within the last 250 years. It is now become a grand literary market, in which the booths and stalls are let at a very high price, even those of the smallest size bringing in a considerable revenue. Here are places of great emolument as well as honour. Large fortunes too are made by the most skilful dealers, and very substantial incomes are acquired by those who continue but a very few years at the mart. The Noblemen and Gentlemen of the Kingdom send their sons here for education, and immense sums of money are obtained by the proprietors of the said booths, not merely for their education, but for their personal accommodation. In fact, the colleges are now subject to the window tax. Every member of the Univ[y] whether *in statu pupillari* or other wise pays this tax, as well as a high price or rent for the apartment or apartments, which he chances to occupy. The servants of Masters and Fellows of colleges gain settlements by service and become parishioners of the parish in which the college is situated, of which they happen to be members. The question therefore is this, are not the owners or occupiers of the colleges liable to be assessed for the property they hold in the Town of Cambridge as well as the rest of the Inhabitants, seeing that they make a profit or advantage of it for their own use & emolument? They have certainly long ceased to be almshouses. If there be a doubt remaining on the subject, let it at once be fairly solved by the Lord Chief Justice of the King's Bench and an English jury. The "honourable men" of the Univ[y] cannot object to this. But I hear some one exclaim, "We are governed by laws of our own. We claim cognizance in our own courts of every thing relating to the Univ[y] except mayhem and treason. Bring the matter before us." This I fear is but too true, and how the Cambridge men will get out of the dilemma I know not. To be judge in one's own cause is such a delightful advantage that no one would give up if he could preserve that and his character at the same time, unless he were a very disinterested sort of a body.

'And here, by the by, good people of England, you need not, indeed you need not, be in the least alarmed at the suspension of the Habeas Corpus act, of which so much has been said. We in Cambridge live and have lived under the suspension of it all our lives. Our houses may be entered at any hour in the day or night without a search warrant by the Univ^y Proctors. We may be sent to the castle, our wives and daughters to the prison, where the common women of the town are confined, we may be discommuned for "shewing any disrespect" not only to "a member of the univ^y" but even to "his servant[1]."

'If we are innkeepers or publicans our licences may at any time be stopped or taken away without assigning any cause. But what then? We are as happy as a litter of pigs in a stye. Is one of our brother pigs destroyed? We make no outcry about it, there is the more milk for those that remain. Were the V. C. to order the house of any one of us to be razed from [*sic*] the ground, we could seek a remedy in no other place than his own court. It is not frequently that these extremes are resorted to. Acts of the species above described have been performed, and we are liable to the repetition every day, but we are Cambridge men, living in the place, and were any one in company to complain of these laws some slave, who battens on the vices of the place, would give you for a toast, "Come here's Cambridge! and they that don't like it, damn 'em, let 'em leave it."

'Observe the time in which these parochial allowances are withdrawn. When the amount of the poor rate and the increase of pauperism is becoming truly alarming. When family after

[1] Note appended to the paper. 'See the Art. Discommuning in Miller, p. 63. This word is not to be found either in Bailey or Johnson's *Dict.* Miller calls it *discommoning.*'

family is obliged to apply to the parish for relief, and those too who a very few years ago never had such a circumstance in contemplation. The tendency of this measure is to add to the sum of both these evils, and that by those who possess immense riches and from whom other and better things might have been fairly expected.'

III. Synopsis of the Contents of the Play.

The play of *Club Law* in the imperfect state in which we have it opens with a scene in which Niphill or Niphle, a prospective Burgomaster of Athens (*sc.* Mayor of Cambridge), makes a compact with a Welchman called Tavie, that for an immoral consideration if Niphle becomes Burgomaster, Tavie shall be made Chief Sergeant. Tavie is at the moment one of three sergeants attending on the Burgomaster, Mr Brecknocke.

Mr Brecknocke comes on the scene and soon after has an apple thrown at his head by a young student named Cricket. The Town Clerk, Spruce, remarks on this, 'By our Ladie but wee must have some remedie against this Club law.' Cricket, who has been chased by the sergeants, in a soliloquy regrets that 'the Welch rogue' had not followed him into the hall (*sc.* College) 'that wee might but had the villaine to the pumpe.' Two older men (whom we may regard as young graduates) Philenius and Musonius come on the scene, and Cricket tells them of his adventure with the Burgomaster. Philenius and Musonius discuss the situation: those who should be their servants 'seeme to be our masters.' Musonius thinks the only remedy is to 'renewe the ancient Club-lawe.' Philenius proposes that they should learn their enemies' secrets by humouring their wives. The next scene shows us the election of a Burgomaster. The outgoing Burgomaster has the names of the 24 electors called over by the Town Clerk. The Town Clerk and the Burgomaster make some diverting speeches and the electors are dismissed to their duties. The result is clear when a cry is heard from within, 'A Niphill! A Niphill!' Niphle is informed of the electors' choice and makes a speech in which he calls on the citizens to help him in punishing 'those stifnecked students.' According to his promise he gives Tavie the place next his person and invites the company to the mayoral feast.

Cricket, determined to deprive Tavie of any share in this entertainment, goes to his house, and by telling him that a countryman of his, one Mr Morgan, wishes to see him, lures him into 'our lodging' (*i.e.* College) where he is locked up and beaten. Another of the sergeants, Puff, invites a Frenchman of the 'Miles Gloriosus' type, Mounsier Grand Combatant, to the Burgomaster's feast, but the Frenchman comes out disgusted with the fare and the company. He prefers 'the Accademick's.' After the feast is over and the electors have left, the Burgomaster and others (*sc.* the Mayor and Aldermen) hold a council to consider the course they are to pursue towards the 'gentle Athenians' (*sc.* members of the University). It is decided that Mr Colby shall forestall the market and carry away their corn ('for you have obteyned your suite'), Mr Rumford shall arrange for them to be well beaten, to 'have their owne Club-lawe,' and Mr Spruce with the assistance of all shall draw up articles embodying their grievances, and a supplication for remedy.

The wives of Colby and Niphle are now made to disclose their discontent with their husbands and their sympathy with the 'gentle Athenians.' They tell Philenius and Musonius that on the following day at a cudgel-play the young lads of the town intend to 'make them feel Club lawe.'

Cricket after playing his trick on Tavie has overheard that Mr Colby is to carry away corn under a load of coals that night. He tells Philenius and Musonius, who, armed with a writ of attachment from Mr Rector (*sc.* the Vice-Chancellor), wait to intercept the operation. Cricket himself fills up time by tying a rope to Mr Burgomaster's door, calling 'murder,' and beating the Burgomaster and his three sergeants when they hurry out and tumble over the rope. He then overhears a private arrangement between Niphle and Tavie that Niphle would visit Tavie's house for an immoral purpose at 12 that night, and would use as a pass-word 'I burn.'

Colby and his colliers are shipping their corn when they are surprised by Musonius, Philenius, Cricket and company. Colby is told of the Rector's writ and is led off to jail, after which Cricket informs Musonius of Niphle's appointment with Tavie. When Musonius goes off to the Rector's to get another writ, Cricket plays another trick on Tavie. By help of Niphle's pass-word 'I burn' he induces Tavie to open his door, and then fells him. Accordingly when Niphle appears himself, he has some difficulty before he is admitted. Musonius has now returned with a writ of search from the Rector, and Philenius from escorting Mr Colby to jail, and they join in demanding admission into Tavie's house. Tavie gives the alarm 'Ho, Mr Nifle, the Rector's search is come, what will you doe?' Niphle manages to escape and hide himself in a tub, in which a poor beggar wench, as it happens, has already taken shelter. He is seen by Cricket—who undertakes to produce him if he is made Captain of the Search. Niphle when found with the beggar woman takes a lofty tone. 'I hope you found me doeinge no ill, but executing my office. Are we not straightly charged to looke to vagabonds and beggars?' However, his remonstrances are disregarded, and he and the woman are carried in their tub to jail.

The inferior members of the search-party are seen in Tavie's house keeping up conversation somewhat unequally with Luce, the supposed sister of Tavie, for whose sake Niphle had visited the house. She is also carried off as a prisoner to the law.

It is nearly morning, and the academics go off to bed.

Rumford in readiness for the attack which is to be made on the 'gentle Athenians' has had staves laid up in Colby's storehouse. Mrs Colby informs Musonius of this, and tells him that he can get them away while the townsmen are drinking. Meanwhile Philenius, who has been to see the Rector, returns with the news that the latter has let Colby out of prison, but has issued bills of discommoning against the leaders of the town.

[*At this point there is a gap in the MS.*]

Tavie has been made Captain of the attacking force, and issues his commands to his natural superiors. Mounsier, though his courage is distrusted by Cricket, joins himself to the other side, who secure the staves from Colby's storehouse.

By way of preparing for the attack, the townsmen arrange fencing-matches between the boys who are with them. Cricket, as directed by his leaders, makes himself offensive and is struck. A general affray then begins. The gentle Athenians bring up their reserve forces, and the townsmen find that their armoury has been rifled. The fight naturally goes against them, Tavie runs away, and the rest beg for forgiveness. Mounsier, however, who has been hiding under a stall, seeing Puff *hors de combat*, attacks him fiercely in revenge for the bad dinner to which Puff had invited him. Cricket who has seen all denounces his cowardice, and the gentle Athenians go to their lodgings (*sc.* College) for the night.

The 5th act shows us the straits to which the townspeople have been reduced by being discommoned. Colby and Rumford have agreed to leave the town and petition the Duke (*sc.* the Queen). Niphle who is now released from jail sees that there is no course open but to submit, but will not be the first to propose it, and suggests that they should complain to the Duke. Brecknocke refuses to carry on the feud any longer, and as the burgesses are clamouring for peace, Colby too gives in. Niphle now proposes a feigned submission and even Rumford, the most fiery spirit, acquiesces. A supplication to the Rector is drawn up by Niphle, on the receipt of which the Rector sends Musonius and Philenius to receive the act of submission. The two emissaries adopt a haughty tone, but promise that if their opponents swear true obedience and service, they shall recover the privileges lost by the discommoning. With the taking of the oath the war is at an end, and Tavie asks Cricket to take him as his true man and servant. Cricket promises to have him made underskinker in the buttery, and then delivers the epilogue.

IV. *Club Law* in its Setting of Time and Place.

1. We have now to discuss the relation in which our play stands to the course of events sketched in Section II. It will be well first to give in full the passage of Fuller's *History of the University of Cambridge*, to which reference was made earlier.

Fuller prefixes to his remarks the following table:

$159\frac{6}{7}$	39	Iohn Iegon Vice can.	William Moon Richard Sutton	Proct.	Robert Wallis Mayor.
$159\frac{7}{8}$	40	Iohn Iegon Vice can.	Nathaniel Cole William Rich	Proct.	James Robson Mayor.

On this it may be remarked that the years denoted $159\frac{6}{7}$, $159\frac{7}{8}$, mean the academical years 1596—7 and 1597—8, the term of office of the Vice-Chancellor beginning in November, that of the Mayor at Michaelmas. The numbers 39, 40 represent the regnal years, the academical year 1596—7 practically coinciding with the 39th and the following year with the 40th year of the reign of Elizabeth. In each of these academical years Dr John Jegon, of Corpus Christi, was Vice-Chancellor, and Robert Wallis was Mayor. James Robson became Mayor at Michaelmas, 1598, and was succeeded at Michaelmas, 1599, by John Yaxley. Fuller errs in putting Robson's mayoralty a year too early[1], and we may well suppose that, as he himself says, he was not specially well acquainted with the municipal history of Cambridge at this period.

Fuller then tells his tale:

'31. The *young Schollars* conceiving themselves somewhat wronged by the *Townsmen* (the particulars whereof I know not) betook them for revenge to their *wits*, as the weapon wherein lay their best advantage. These having gotten a discovery of some

[1] Fuller's mistake is reproduced by his editors, though Wright claims to have corrected Fuller's catalogue of mayors by the books of the Corporation. See list of mayors, etc. in Camb. Univ. Library MS. Ff. III. 33 (17), the accuracy of which is abundantly confirmed.

Town privacies, from *Miles Goldsborrough*[1] (one of their own Corporation) composed a merry (but abusive) *Comedy* (which they call'd CLUB-LAW) in *English*, as calculated for the capacities of such, whom they intended *spectatours* thereof. *Clare-Hall* was the place wherein it was acted, and the Major, with his Brethren, and their Wives, were invited to behold it, or rather themselves abused therein. A convenient place was assigned to the *Towns-folk* (rivetted in with *Schollars* on all sides) where they might see and be seen. Here they did behold themselves in their own best cloathes (which the Schollars had borrowed) so livelily personated, their *habits*, *gestures*, *language*, *lieger-jests*, and *expressions*, that it was hard to decide, which was the *true Townsman*, whether he that *sat by*, or he who *acted on the Stage*. *Sit still* they could not for *chafing*, *go out* they could not for *crowding*, but impatiently patient were fain to attend till dismissed at the end of the *Comedy*.

'32. The *Major* and his *Brethren* soon after complain of this *libellous Play* to the *Lords* of the *Privie Councell*, and truly aggravate the *Scollars offence*, as if the *Majors Mace* could not be played with, but that the *Scepter* it selfe is touched therein. Now, though such the *gravity* of the *Lords*, as they must *maintain Magistracy*, and not behold it *abused*: yet such their *goodness*, they would not with too much *severity* punish *Wit*, though *waggishly*

[1] Miles Goldesborough, whose name appears among the 'Four and Twenty' chosen on 4th December, 1599 (see p. xxvii), was a baker. The *Acta Curiæ* of the University show that on 7th April, 1598, the University taxers accused 'Milonem Gouldesboroughe,' Baker, of giving short weight. He confessed and was condemned in iii^s iv^d and 'one great Browne loaf for the poore prisoners in the castle & Tolboothe' and in costs. From evidence given before the Vice-Chancellor in the case of William Nicholson on 14th October, 1597, and now preserved in MS. 37. 2 (53 f.) in the University Registry, it would seem that Goldesborough held another office as well. Collinson the jailer deposed 'Prettie and Hurst were delivered to prison this day fortnight upon an execution and the same night lett oute againe, for the same night they sent a caution, viz. a silver cuppe, to Mr Miles Gouldesboroughe, Bailiff of the Tolbooth [the town jail on the south side of the Market-place, see Atkinson and Clark, *Cambridge Described*, pp. 82—95], for his indemnitie and to dischardge that for which they were laid in in execution, and the said Mr Miles Gouldesboroughe did saie to me "You may inlardge them."'

imployed; and therefore only sent some *slight* and *private check* to the *principall Actors* therein.

'33. There goeth a *tradition*, many earnestly engaging for the *truth* thereof, that the *Townsmen* not contented herewith, importunately pressed, That *some more severe and publick punishment might be inflicted upon them.* Hereupon, the *Lords* promised in short time to come to *Cambridge*, and (because the *life* in such things is lacking when onely *read*) they themselves would *see* the same *Comedy*, with all the *properties* thereof, *acted over again*, (the *Townsmen* as formerly, being enjoyned to be *present thereat*) that so they might the better proportion the *punishment* to the *fault*, if any appeared. But rather than the *Townsmen* would be *witnesses* again to their own *abusing*, (wherein many things were *too farre from*, and some things *too near to truth*) they fairly fell off from any farther prosecution of the matter.'

2. Was Fuller right in assigning the play of *Club Law* either to the year 1597—8 or to the mayoralty of Robson 1598—9?

Hawkins, in his edition of *Ignoramus* (1787), p. xvi, says that *Club Law* was acted 'in 1597—8 as Fuller affirms, but according to other authorities in 1599.' Who the 'other authorities' were, I do not know. Possibly Hawkins is giving the view of Dr Farmer, who, as we have argued, had a manuscript of our play. At any rate someone or other in the 18th century suspected an error in the date given by Fuller—and I believe with good reason.

In my view the performance of the play *Club Law* took place in the mayoralty of John Yaxley, that is, in the year 1599—1600, and, perhaps probably, at the beginning of that mayoral year.

I come to this conclusion because I believe Niphle to represent Yaxley; Brecknocke, Wallis; Tavie, Hugh Jones; and Colby, William Nicholson.

3. Of Niphle, we are told 'his father was Baker, he brought him up pretelie to his booke, hee is a pretie petifogging Lawyer, a kinde of Attorney, hel'e drawe bloud of theise gentle Athenians' (l. 462). He enters on office with a determination to outdo his predecessors in hostility towards the academics.

John Yaxley, whose hostility to the University we have seen, was a lawyer and very probably the son of a baker. At any rate there was a baker of the same name in Cambridge at this time[1].

As to John Yaxley, the Mayor, Bowtell in his MS. History of Cambridge preserved at Downing College, mentions John Yaxley in connexion with St Edward's parish, but adds: 'Yaxley lived sometime in St Michael's parish and kept the Rose-tavern which he quitted in 1609 for a residence at Waterbeach, where being a lawyer, he became steward to the Prince's court. He founded an almshouse at Waterbeach for six poor widows...as it appeareth by his will, proved in the Commons, A.D. 1628.'

A contemporary document lent by Dr Farmer to Cole and transcribed in Cole MSS. vol. 51 (Add. MSS. 5852, fo. 89) has the following:

'Camb. Maij 22, 1598. Names of such Persons dwellinge in St Michaells Parish as are able to give Relieffe to the Poore of the same parishe weekly—Mr Yaxley vi^{d}' [no one else above iiij^{d}].

Further in the *State Papers*, Domestic Series, James I, vol. LVII., we have some light thrown on Yaxley's later proceedings:

'Sep. 3 [1610]. Examinations of Roger Woodall, Mark Charlton and Richard Bankes concerning misdemeanours of John Yaxley, steward of the manor of Waterbeach.

'Sep. 11. [Earl of Salisbury] to Sir Hen. Fanshaw to draw a commission for examination of the misdemeanours of John Yaxley, and of Rob. Spicer [his son-in-law] deputy steward.'

[1] On 15th December, 1598, the Inferior Bedell, Ben. Pryme, accused 'Joh. Yaxley de Cant. Pistorem' of giving short weight. A similar charge was made against him on 7th December, 1599, and it was affirmed 'that ye said Yaxley had and hath so offended in ffive severall batches.' He was condemned in xii^{s} vi^{d}. Like charges were made against him on 14th March, $1\frac{599}{600}$, and on 23rd May, 1600. (*Acta Curiæ.*) The Corporation Accounts, 'Libri rationales III.' (preserved at Downing College) have under 1597 the following note of money received:

'it: of Mr Yaxley for the farme of Sturbridge land liii^{s} iiii^{d}.'

This is probably the baker. Cp. Cooper, II. 563 bot.

On the evidence of Mark Charlton, Yaxley was charged *inter alia* with appropriating to his own use town lands of Waterbeach, and afterwards compounding with the churchwardens to receive £40 for them; also with compounding with one Edward Banks for £10 not to join with the tenants in claiming the lands. It was stated that 'one John Haselop of Trumpington friend to M[r] Yaxley beareth the name of Bayley to the Kings Manor of Waterbeach, but M[r] Yaxley and Rob. Spicer his son in law do jointlie execute the office.' Reference is made to Mr Yaxley's 'owne house in Cambridge.'

One incident in the play—Niphle's detection by members of the University when visiting a house late at night for an immoral purpose, and his plea that he was 'executing his office' (Act III. Sc. 8, ll. 1522 etc.) might, taken alone, make us disposed to identify Niphle with Wallis rather than with Yaxley. At any rate it seems to have been suggested by something that occurred in the early days of Wallis' mayoralty and that is related in the articles of complaint against the University of 13th November, 1596:

'*Item*, the Maior going out to represse misdemeanors offered by divers younge men of the Universitye and to see the Quenes peace keptt was assalted and evel intreated by three or fower Schollers, and his gowne rent and spoiled, and some used lewde speeches to the Maior and he putt in danger of his lyf.'

But it would be natural for the University satirists to attach to the Mayor of the time being any scandalous story told of a former Mayor, and it is possible that something similar had occurred to Yaxley himself.

Yaxley is said by Cole to have died about 1628.

4. Of Brecknocke, we hear that he has been Burgomaster two years (l. 2441), that unlike Niphle he lives by his merchandize (l. 2456), is a chandler (l. 146), that though Niphle now finds him backward in resisting the foes of the town, he has been forward in times past (l. 2453).

The only man in these years who had been Mayor of Cambridge twice was Robert Wallis, who had been elected in

1596 and 1597, and had been a determined opponent of University privileges[1]. It would be natural however in a play written against Yaxley, to represent Yaxley as intending to eclipse his predecessor Wallis.

One may perhaps find an additional piece of evidence for identifying Brecknocke with Wallis, in Brecknocke's words (l. 2658), 'We must [stand bareheaded] being in petition. doe you not knowe last yeare when I was Burgomaster Sir Obedus Tuck stood bare headed to mee? Much more must wee.' I suggest that by 'Sir Obedus Tuck' is meant no less a person than Sir Thomas North, the translator of Plutarch, and refer to the accounts of the town, presented at Michaelmas, 1598, for the year then ending, *i.e.* the second year of Wallis' mayoralty, 'Item, paid to Sir Thomas Northe Knight for a benevolence from ye towne xx^{li}[2].'

If, however, Wallis is meant by Brecknocke (whose name may well have been suggested by 'Wallis' or 'Wales'), there is a departure from historical accuracy when Niphle (= Yaxley) is made Brecknocke's immediate successor in the mayoralty. No mention is made of James Robson, who was Mayor between Wallis and Yaxley. This may be accounted for on the ground that Robson, as we have seen[3], was less hostile to the University than his predecessor and his successor, and was therefore spared the castigation which they received. It is possible that he is 'Mr Shavett' (l. 458).

There is a further difficulty in that while Robson was a chandler[4], Wallis does not appear to have been one. In a

[1] He had been chosen an Alderman on 4th October, 1594 (Metcalfe MS. Downing Coll.).

[2] Cooper, II. 593. Sir Thos. North was a brother of Roger Lord North and according to the *D.N.B.* was always in reduced circumstances. His translation of Plutarch's Lives appeared in 1579. He is thought to have been educated at Peterhouse, was knighted about 1591, and was in the commission of the peace for the County of Cambridge in 1592 and 1597. In 1601 he received a pension of £40 per annum from the Queen, and appears to have died soon after.

[3] p. xxv.

[4] A Covenant Bond, in the office of the Town Clerk, Cambridge, of 6th January, 25 Eliz. (158$\frac{2}{3}$), is signed 'Jas. Robson burg. et chandeler.'

document published by Cooper (II. pp. 595, 596) he is seen dealing in coal and rye. We also find him in 1600 paying rent to the Corporation for 'Nevenham [Newnham] Mills and the close and meadow thereunto belonging l^{li}[1].'

On the whole however I believe that in Brecknocke the author of the play intended to satirize Wallis.

Wallis was again elected to the mayoralty in 1606 at the end of the year of office of John Edmonds deceased. He is said by Bowtell[2] to have died about 1624.

5. Tavie is one of the three sergeants in attendance on the Burgomaster Brecknocke when the play opens (ll. 30—36). He is especially obnoxious to the gentle Athenians (ll. 114—116). He is an inn-keeper at whose house one may play 'tables' (ll. 580, 1992—2001, 2806—7) and his house has a bad repute (l. 21, etc.). He condemns himself in the end for having forsaken 'his old master,' and declares on being promised by Cricket the place of 'under skinker in the buttery' that he will not do so again (l. 2836).

Hugh Jones, as we have seen[3], though a dismissed servant of the University and a person very obnoxious to that body, had been made one of the sergeants by Wallis. We learn the following further particulars about him from the *Acta Curiæ* of the University.

On the 4th and 11th March, 159$\frac{6}{7}$, a suit was brought by Thos. Turner, M.A., St John's College, against Hugh Jones. It was decreed that Jones should be arrested and kept in safe custody.

'27 May, 1597. Hilliard and Bowlton Proctors...con Hug. Joanes. It was alleged that "Joanes did lodge or suffered to be lodged in his howse certaine Schollers and suffered them to playe at the tables cardes and dyce in his howse." [Joanes denied the offence but it was found "omnia esse vera."] "quia sufficienter sibi constabat of the greate and continuall disorder that hathe bene

[1] *Libri Rationales*, III. (Downing College).

[2] MS. Hist. of Cambridge (Downing College).

[3] p. xxi.

and ys daielye vsed and kepte in his howse decrevit dictum Joanes sub salva custodia custodiri donee [he found security] to keepe good order and vsage in his howse, [and in default of security] that the saide Joanes shalbe dischardged from keepeing of an Inne and from victuallinge likewise. Et paulo post Dno adhuc *pro* tribunali seden. Dni procuratores pred. allegaverunt that they even nowe doe come from the saide Hughe Joanes his howse, and when they were there, they fownde some playeinge at the tables there, and have broughte from thence the tables they played withall and shewed them in open Courte and alledged that one John Banbridge a Cook did playe at the tables there with another et...introduxerunt pd. Johnem Banbridge et Georgium Bubworthe qui affirmaverunt allegata pd. esse vera, sayeinge that the said John Banbridge and one Richard Gilman servaunte to Mr Milner of Trinitye Colledge did playe there at the tables even righte nowe for beere breade and cheese.

'Dñus...condemnavit pr. Joanes in xl*s*.....'

On 8th July, 1597, the Proctors brought a suit against Hugh Jones, of Cambridge, 'Inhoulder,' alleging that 'he keepeth an Inne in Cambridge and did dresse fleshe uppon a fastinge daye, viz. Midsomer even last past.' It was ordered that 'the said Joanes hereafter shall keepe good rule in his howse,' etc.

On 7th October, 1597, the Proctors sue Hugh Jones and others, alleging 'that they...have dressed fleshe upon dayes prohibited.'

On 7th April, 1598, it is ordered that 'Hugonem Joanes arestari et secure custodiri' in the matter of a debt of £7 5*s*.

On 15th February, 1$\frac{599}{600}$, 'Hughe Joanes' of 'the George' is included in a list of the 'Hostellarii and Vitellarii' of the town.

On 18th July, 1600, George Scarlette, Bachelor in Arts, sued Hugh Jones. On the 19th Jones said 'Scarlette first callinge him knave, he the said Joanes said to this viz. "he is a knave that calls me knave."' The Vice-Chancellor decreed that Jones 'secure custodiri in carcere vocat. Cambridge Castle et non alibi donee solverit seu satisfecerit p*rae*fato Scarletto...tam quoad summam xx^{s}...quam quoad summam xv^{s}...in toto xxxv^{s}.'

On 24th July, 1600, George Scarlet of St John's College sued Thomas Creame. Scarlet stated that after the preceding case Jones was committed to Thomas Creame to be kept in custody and that he was then liberated 'iniuria et negligentia i*mpri*mis Thomæ Creame,' who 'did leave the said Hugh Joanes at the said Castle and tooke no further care to advise to Mr Vichancellar what further course he would take for the due execution to be made againste the saide Hughe Joanes for the paymente of the saide xxxv^s eaque ratione Joanes liberatus fuit et est.' Creame confessed the allegations to be true and was condemned to Scarlet for the sum of xxxv^s aforesaid.

Jones is also mentioned in the case of W. Nicholson tried before the Vice-Chancellor on 14th October, 1597[1]:

'Then Mr Vicechancellor being desirous to knowe howe the said Prettie and Hurst came to prison againe—of themselves—or by themselves, W. Nicholson answeared, He that had them oute of prison at the ffirste broughte them to prison againe this daie, and that was Hugge Joanes the Sargeante.'

6. Of Colby we are told in the play, 'You Mr Colebie shall forestall the market and carrie away their Corne for you have obteyned your suite' (ll. 718—720). He is detected by the University authorities in carrying away corn, is imprisoned, but is released quickly by the Rector 'upon small consideration' (l. 1925), or according to Colby's account, 'it cost my purse soundly' (l. 1988). In Colby we can hardly fail to see William Nicholson[2], who had been fined in 1596 for ingrossing corn, had been imprisoned in the Castle, but shortly escaped, had had a writ of *habeas corpus* served on the Vice-Chancellor, and had finally won a suit for false imprisonment in Trinity term 1599, which involved the Vice-Chancellor and the Inferior Bedell, Pryme, in heavy money loss and had consigned the latter to prison for inability to pay. He had been chosen Alderman on 12th April, 1597[3].

[1] MS. in the University Registry, 37. 2 (53 f.).

[2] Colby is addressed by Rumford as 'billie Coleby' (l. 2493), but it is possible that 'billie' is the Scotch or Northern word = 'fellow,' 'comrade,' and not the familiar form of the Christian name.

[3] Metcalfe MS. (Downing Coll.).

7. If these identifications be accepted, it is natural to suppose that *Club Law* was acted soon after Yaxley had become Mayor, and when the violence of his proceedings against the University led certain students to think that the proper way of dealing with him and his fellows was to discommon them. There is no evidence that Yaxley was discommoned, as a matter of fact, though Edmonds had been discommoned in his mayoralty thirteen years before, and other Mayors were to be discommoned in later times. The play was a suggestion to the authorities, but the suggestion was not acted on.

Another argument for our dating of the play may be found in the fact that we hear of no complaint made on the part of the town against University plays until we come to a document of which we have a copy in Baker's hand in MS. Harl. 7047, fol. 83. It is headed: 'An abstract of some town complaints, with the University answeres. Anno 1601.' Here the complaint runs: 'The scholers of the University, being in taverns, alehouses and diverse publick places, do grievously and very disorderly misuse in generall all free burgesses, and in particular the magistrates of the town. And also in the Plays in colleges and publick sermons, whereby great occasion of grudge is offered.'

8. To turn from the special evidence of date to more general points.

Henry Spruce is no doubt a portrait of the Town Clerk, Henry Slegge (elected about 1596[1]), and possibly the speech put in Spruce's mouth (l. 329, etc.) is a parody of Mr Slegge's oratory. There seems to be a reference to the same gentleman in the character of orator in the *Returne from Parnassus*, Part I. (1600), l. 497, where the Tailor is speaking of students: 'They shoulde shewe good examples to others, as our towne clarke shewed verie learnedly in an oration he made.' It is clear that Rumford and Cipher and the sergeants Puff and Catch are portraits of actual persons; but I do not find it possible to identify them[2]. Cipher had once been

[1] Cooper, III. 41.

[2] 'Thomas Knevett the Sargeante' is mentioned as 'coming in Mr Maiors name' in the case of W. Nicholson, 14th October, 1597 (MS. in University Registry, 37. 2 (53 f.)).

Burgomaster (l. 2669), and may be John Edmunds (Mayor 1586—7) or Thomas Metcalfe (Mayor 1592)[1]. Rumford was a headsman[2] and a butcher (ll. 2548, 2596) who spoke a north-country dialect, and who would seem to have had a grievance against the University in connexion with the prohibition of dressing flesh in Lent (l. 2077, which is however very obscure). Alderman William Wulfe was a butcher[3], but there were other Wulfes in Cambridge, and this makes it improbable that he was a north-countryman. He had been Mayor in 1589 and died in 160$\frac{0}{1}$, being buried in the chapel of Trinity Hall on 5th March[4]. He was probably therefore not so young or vigorous a man as Rumford is represented to have been. Mr 'Thirtens' (l. 261), one of the Four and Twenty, is clearly Godfrey Twelves[5], who is in the list of the Four and Twenty chosen in 1599, and similarly Mr 'Silverburrowe' is 'Miles Goldsborow,' of whom we have heard. Mr 'Westcocks' would seem to be John Norkot, but the latter was an Alderman and ex-Mayor, not a member of the Four and Twenty.

Probably Mrs Niphle and Mrs Colby had some prototypes in the Cambridge of three hundred years ago; and the rather colourless but well-meaning Musonius and Philenius may be typical of many young dons of the day.

9. The picture of life and manners given in *Club Law* is a highly-coloured one, and one must not treat it too seriously. One feels however that it does give us something of the spirit of the stirring days in which it was written.

One of the most lively incidents is the election of a Burgomaster. It is worth while therefore to give a document which shows us the

[1] See p. xxv.

[2] *i.e.* a member of the Corporation.

[3] A Covenant Bond, preserved in the office of the Town Clerk, Cambridge, of 21st September, 25 Eliz. (1583), is signed 'Willm. Wulfe, burg. et butcher,' and the *Acta Curiæ* of 11th November, 1597, include a suit brought by the Proctors against 'Willm. Wolfe Lanium Aldermannum.'

[4] Registers of St Edward's parish, quoted by Cole.

[5] He was an apothecary (Cooper, III. 42). His burial is given in St Peter's Register under 14th November, 1626 (Cole). The name 'Twelves' in the next generation became 'Twells.'

very curious manner in which a Mayor of Cambridge was elected at this time. The document, which dates probably from 1592, is contained in Metcalfe's *Thesaurus* preserved at Downing College.

'An order made by the lord North high Steward of the Towne of Cambridge for electinge the mayo^r^ balives and other officers within the same Towne.

'This daie & Yere by a common assent & by thadvice of the right honorable the lord north high steward of the Towne of Cambridge is an order made for the electinge of the mayo^r^ baylives & other officers yeerly vsed to bee choosen within this Towne the tenor of wch order followethe in theise wordes viz

'Imprimis that euerie of the xxiiii^tie^ or so many of them as shall be presente in the hall shall write his name in a litle peace of paper and the same shall laye downe upon the table before the mayo^r^ & aldermen wch names so written · shalbee enclosed in seuerall balls of wax of one color & like quantity by such two aldermen as the mayor shall appointe and the same so enclosed in wax shalbee put into a box by the said two aldermen and that done the mayo^r^ and aldermen then present or the more parte of them shall appointe one alderman to take out one ball for the bench and the comons shall appoint one comoner to take forth another ball for them & those ij persones whose names are in the said ii balls shall chose xii persones p*ar*cell of thelleccõn that is to saie iii persones in euerie warde And if one of the xxiiii^tie^ be absent then hee or they so absent to beare no office for the yere to come.

'Itm. the said ii persones so chosen & sworne shall goe together into some place w^th^in the house & shall choose xii persones to bee of theleccõn of wch two and twelve persones none shall bee eligible to beare anie office of baylive for the yere to come And yf the two cannot agree of the choosinge of the said Twelve then eyther partie to choose six. And this to bee done w^th^in one houre next after there goeinge togeather the same houre to bee tryed by an houre glasse vpon payne of forfeyture euery man makinge default iii^li^ vi^s^ viii^d^ to bee levied to thuse of the Towne.

'Itm. that the said Twelve thus gathered together & sworne or the more parte of them shall chuse unto them six more persones to make up the number of eighteene persones whereof none shall bee eligible to beare anie office of baylif for the yere to come wthin one hour next after ther goeinge together upon payne of forfeyture every man making defalt xx^{s} And if the said xii persones cannot agree wthin the said Houre to bee tryed as afforesaid then the more parte of the said persones to name the same six euerie of them to give his voice vpon payne of xx^{s} And yf equallty of voices doe chaunce then the said xii persones shall write the names of those six persones whome they would haue & laye them downe vpon the table before the mayo^{r} and then the mayo^{r} to have the castinge voice

'And if those eighteene men so choosen sworne and gathered together cannot agree wthin one houre next after meeting then the more parte them to take place[1] And if equallity of voices doe chaunce then the mayo^{r} likwise to haue the castinge voice in manner and forme as ys afforesaid

'The oth of the sworne electors

'Yee shall swere that since thestablishinge of this order for eleccon of officers you haue not labored nor bene labored vnto directly or indirectly to bringe anie man to office for this yere to come or to lett or hinder anie man from anie office for this yere to come vnto wch labo^{r} you haue directly or indirectlie given your assent consent or promise so help you god, etc.'

After the election the Burgomaster invited the Aldermen and Four and Twenty to a feast. This was in accordance with Cambridge custom. Who paid for the feast when Yaxley was elected in 1599 is not clear, but a minute of the Corporation made on 17th July, 1600, runs as follows: 'It is agreed by a comon assent that the supper vsually to bee kept hereafter on the daie of eleccon of the maior and Baylives shalbee borne by the maior and baylives that shall be then elected[2].' Possibly till then it had been borne by the Mayor solely.

We are told that Niphle, expecting to be made Mayor, 'hath

[1] There is some corruption here.

[2] Metcalfe's *Thesaurus* (Downing College).

bought him a satten sute all readie.' A minute of 13th January, 1559, runs, 'all chosen to the benche shall have and weare murreye gownes and tippetts'; one of 7th October, 1560, 'every maior...to buy for his wife one scarlett gowne'; and one of 15th December, 1575, 'the maior to wear his scarlet gowne [on fixed days][1].'

The three sergeants who attend on the Mayor are true to fact. A paper in the Baker MSS.[2] shows us their duties:

'The oathe of the sarieante.

'Ye shall sweare that you shall geve diligent attendaunce upon Mr Maior of this towne duringe the tyme of yor office and true execution make of all writts warrants and precepts to you directed by Mr Maior or any of the Quenes Justice of her peace wthin this Towne of Camebridge and the libertyes of the same And true retorne of the same make and delyver And of all the Custome and towle that ye shall take or Receave by the Reason of yor said offices And shall make a trew accompt to the said Maior and Bayliffs And all other thinges that be apperteining to yor office you shall well and trewly do and execute duringe this year to come. So help, etc.'

From the history given earlier we can see that the author of the play is drawing no fancy picture when he shows the Rector or Vice-Chancellor issuing one writ for arresting a forestaller or ingrosser of corn and another for searching a house of ill-repute. The drawing up of articles of complaint against the University (ll. 728—775, 2383, 2415, 2437) had been a common incident in the wars of town and gown, and the oath taken by the Mayor to preserve the University's privileges (ll. 2599—2603, 2771—2798) a chief bone of contention. And we have seen cases before in which students met their opponents with the 'argumentum baculinum' or club-law.

Municipal oratory is a stock-subject for academic wit, and the speeches pronounced by Brecknocke (ll. 362 etc.) and Niphle (ll. 482 etc., 2568 etc., 2711 etc.) have their analogues in the

[1] Metcalfe's *Thesaurus* (Downing College).

[2] Camb. Univ. Lib. MS. Ff. III. 33.

Returne from Parnassus, Part II., where we have the speech of a Mayor (ll. 1849 etc.) and one of a Burgess (ll. 528 etc.). Brecknocke's proposal that the 'gentle Athenians' shall be brought to marry the daughters of townsmen (l. 681) reminds us that the University had complained of the townsmen for drawing students into clandestine marriages[1]. We get further glimpses into the life of Cambridge at this time when we see a tutor wearing a dagger (ll. 1369 etc.), members of the University—as in *Pedantius* and the Parnassus Plays—heavily in debt to Cambridge tradesmen (l. 2597), townsmen at a cudgel-play (ll. 2093 etc.), the duties of a college servant (l. 2828), and the subjection of young students to the punishment of 'breeching' (l. 136). There is even a modern ring about Cricket's cry, 'Theise Tutors are such troublesome things' (l. 122). In the references to 'an iniquitie' (l. 1916), to Orlando Furioso and Lais (ll. 1662, 1663), we see the interest which was taken in contemporary drama within the little world of the University.

10. On the other hand there are certain characters in the play whose prototypes we shall seek rather in the world at large than in the little world of town and gown.

Mounsier Grand Combatant belongs to the genus 'Miles Gloriosus' which is so frequently represented in comedy from Plautus downwards. Luce is the typical courtesan, drawn with more than ordinary verve. The boy-undergraduate Cricket has something of the character of the Vice in the Moralities. 'Spoiling' for a fight, chafing at being treated as a boy, equal to all occasions, good-natured when approached with sufficient humility, he gives life to the whole play[2].

The various perversions of the Queen's English indulged in by the Frenchman, Mounsier, the Welchman, Tavie, and the Northerner, Rumford, are part of the stock-in-trade of English comic writers. The French-English dialect appears in the *Returne from Parnassus*, Part II., in the mouth of Theodore, in *Three Ladies of London* (1584), *Three Lords and Three Ladies of London* (1590)

[1] Cp. p. xxix.

[2] A merry fellow bears the name 'Will Crickett' in *Wily Beguil'd*.

and *Triumphs of Love and Fortune* (1589), all in Hazlitt-Dodsley, vol. VI., in Shakespeare's *Henry V* (1599) (Queen Katharine and Alice) and in Dekker's *Old Fortunatus* (1600), *Wonder of a Kingdom* (1636), etc. The Welch-English combination appears in *A Hundred Mery Tales* (1526), LXI., in Shakespeare's *Merry Wives* (1597—8) (Sir Hugh Evans) and *Henry V* (1599) (Fluellen), and in Dekker's *Satiro-mastix* (1602) (Sir Vaughan). Northern-English is exemplified in R. Greene's *James the Fourth* (before 1592) (Bohan), *The Pleasant Historie of Thomas of Reading* (before 1600) (Hodgekins of Halifax, etc.) and in *Conflict of Conscience* (Hazlitt-Dodsley, VI.) (Caconos).

As will be seen by the Notes, the language of the ordinary speakers in the play contains many expressions which are either not found in the *New English Dictionary* or not attested for so early a date. The very word 'Club-law' seems to make its first appearance in this play.

11. Whether *Club Law* had any important consequences, beyond providing an evening's entertainment, I am doubtful. Fuller's story taken as a story is all that one could wish, but I am not sure that he would wish us to treat it as history. It seems to me very improbable that the actors should have been able to borrow the clothes of the townspeople whom they were caricaturing; and a little unlikely that they should have induced them to come to Clare Hall to see the play[1]. As to the complaints to the Privy Council and the Privy Council's humorous reply, one can only say that the Acts of the Privy Council as published make no mention of *Club*

[1] The fact that *Club Law* is in English may be thought to support the theory that it was written to be understood by townspeople. Certainly the great majority of plays acted in colleges were in Latin, and in 1592 the Vice-Chancellor, Dr Still, and the Heads wrote to Lord Burleigh, 'Englishe Comedies, for that we never used any, wee presentlie have none,' and accordingly asked leave to present a play before the Queen in Latin. But the English comedy, *Gammer Gurton's Needle*, had been performed probably in 1566, two English plays were produced at Trinity in 1559 (Bursar's Book), another, *Ezechias*, had been acted before the Queen at King's in 1564, and the *Pilgrimage to Parnassus* had been given at St John's at Christmas 1598, to be followed by the two parts of *The Returne from Parnassus* in 1600 and 1602. And *Lingua* had perhaps been acted before the date of *Club Law*.

Law. Mr Mullinger indeed, in his *History of the University of Cambridge*, treats the play as a *causa mali*[1]; to me, it seems that it was only an incident in a contest in which very serious matters were at stake. It is remarkable that when the town, as we have seen[2], did complain in 1601 that 'the scholers of the university...misuse in generall all free burgesses and in particular the magistrates of the town, And also in the plays in colleges and publick sermons,' the heads of the University stoutly denied the fact. 'Whereas it is alledged that the scholers in the playes and sermons misuse the burgesses and magistrates of the town, they affirm the same to be most untrue, malitious and slanderous; neither do they know any abuse offered, except on the 23rd of April, certain young gentlemen and scholers, being in a tavern, did misbehave themselves in speeches towards the maior and his brethren passing by the said tavern; for which offence they were punished and censured by the vice-chancellor and Mr Dr Nevill, dean of Canterbury.' Could such a denial have been made if the writers had ever heard of the performance of *Club Law*? or, at any rate, if the performance had created anything like a public scandal?

V. Authorship of the Play.

The play of *Club Law* may well be considered anonymous.

It has been ascribed however to George Ruggle, who in 1598 removed from Trinity College to Clare Hall, was elected to a Fellowship, and in 1615 made himself famous as the author of the Latin comedy *Ignoramus*. In his edition of *Ignoramus* (1787),

[1] 'The unfortunate burgesses, full of sullen resentment, would seem, for a long time afterwards, to have eagerly seized on every opportunity that presented itself for alleging some wrong, real or imaginary, suffered at the hands of the University. There is still extant a formal statement of these grievances which they caused to be drawn up in the year 1601' (II. p. 442).

'Dr J. Jegon...was vice-chancellor in the year when Club Law was acted, and was again elected, for the third time, two years later....It is not improbable that the townsmen may have been resolved to make him sensible of their displeasure at the special affront to which they had been subjected during his tenure of office' (p. 443).

[2] p. xlviii.

p. lxxi, Mr J. S. Hawkins tells us that in a copy of *Ignoramus* which in 1741 belonged to Mr John Hayward, a Master of Arts in Clare Hall, he had read the following note in Mr Hayward's hand: 'N.B. Mr. Geo. Ruggle wrote besides two other comedies, Revera or Verily, and Club Law, to expose the puritans, not yet printed. MS.' Mr Hawkins continues very sensibly: 'By the letters "MS." at the end, it is imagined Mr. *Hayward* intended to express that he derived this intelligence from some manuscript authority: but, as he has not mentioned where it was to be then found, there does not seem sufficient evidence to support his assertion.'

As to Mr Hayward's statement, the play *Revera or Verily* (the only one of the two which could have been written 'to expose the Puritans') is lost. It is not clear whether it was in Latin or English, probably in Latin. It does not seem to me impossible that *Club Law* should have been written by Ruggle, especially if it is to be dated in 1599 or 1600, after Ruggle had become domiciled at Clare. But it is impossible to use internal evidence to prove the common authorship of two works so utterly different as *Club Law* and *Ignoramus*; and we are left to the authority of Mr Hayward's MS., which may be valuable or may not.

In his preface to the *Parnassus Plays*, the Rev. W. D. Macray states that Francis Brakyn, the Deputy Recorder (afterwards Recorder) of Cambridge—who is supposed to have been Ruggle's butt in *Ignoramus*—'had already been satirized in *Club Law*.' If it were so, it might be taken as some slight evidence of common authorship. There is, however, no ground for this statement, so far as I can see, and it is unfortunate that it has been perpetuated in the *New English Dictionary* (*s.v.* 'Club law').

Other evidence of common authorship might be found in the fact that the author of *Club Law* (according to Fuller) and the author of *Ignoramus* (according to Hawkins[1]) alike derived some of their information from Mr Miles Goldesborough, one of the Four and Twenty. Hawkins gives no authority, however, for his statement, and it may be due to some vague recollection on his part, or someone else's, of what Fuller had said in regard to *Club Law*.

[1] p. xv.

CLUB LAW.

DRAMATIS PERSONÆ.

Mr BRECKNOCKE, Burgomaster of Athens.

PETER BRECKNOCKE, his son.

Mr NICHOLAS NIPHLE, Brecknocke's successor as Burgomaster.

Mris NIPHLE.

Mr HENRY SPRUCE, Town Clerk.

Mr COLBY
Mr RUMFORD } 'Headsmen' or members of the Corporation.
Mr CIPHER

Mris COLBY.

JOCKY RUMFORD, Rumford's son.

Electors for the Burgomastership:

Mr SIXPENNY
Mr LITTLEWORTH
Mr HALFECAKE
Goodman COWBY
Mr ASSELEY
Mr LOBSON
Goodman KETLEBASEN
Mr THIRTENS
Mr MOONE the elder
Mr SILVERBURROWE
Mr ESDRAS
Mr FFESCU
Mr MALLICE
Goodman HORNESBIE
Mr WESTCOCKS
Goodman OLIVER GOOSTURD
Mr JONAS
Goodman NIXON
Goodman COOPERBURNE
Goodman ROGER COWPER
Mr ANDERTON
Mr SLUGG
Goodman GALLANT
Goodman TONGUE IT.

TAVIE, PUFF, TOM CATCH: Sergeants in attendance on the Burgomaster.

PHILENIUS, MUSONIUS: 'Academics' of standing.

NICHOLAS CRICKET, a young student.

PURCUS, BROMLY, ROGER TROTT, SPONER: Searchers in the service of the Rector.

Mounsier GRAND COMBATANT, a Frenchman.

LUCE, a courtesan.

A beggar-wench.

Three colliers or porters (*i.e.* 'coalheavers').

FFOOTS, ADAM: townsmen.

Students, townspeople &c.

[CLUB LAW]

(The fragments give the beginnings of lines on the recto sides, and the ends of lines on the verso sides of the leaves.)

Cover	blank ?		
leaf 2	blank ?		
leaf 3 recto (page 1)		rward	leaf 3 verso (page 2)
		ng	
		Huff	
leaf 4 recto (page 3) ? here the play begins	d	n	leaf 4 verso (page 4)
	Ile		
	r		
	K	I	
	I		
	b	t	
		u	
		mt	
		ome	
	Bre	or-	
	Spe	se, but	
	Ad	would	
	wh		
	bu	p	
	Co		
	wh	r	
	sn	er	
	s.	I	

you t

ha u
son
I co I
work I
Burg h
I stay for the
be good y, Ile
Peter would
serve

leaf 5 recto (page 5) at bottom

leaf 5 verso (page 6)

p
th e
w ,

for our may day, that ever you heard, but I must about my busines, I must tell my master, the Serjeants will come, and the brome man will be here on Saterdaye, they that are bound must obey. p. 7

ACTUS 1us. Scena 4^a^.

Niphill. Tavie.

Nip. Before god Tavie, wellfare thy good heart, I had not thought welshmen had byn so honest, shee was a bounching wench, a smoker effaith.

Tavie. her ferie glad her arships turne her as

never taught no forsooth, may her arships tell her as her holesome?

Nip. ffaith as sweete as a nutt, a good naturd girle I tell thee Tavie, I had as leve as an 100l. my wife were of as good constitution.

Tav. Her hope her arships as tinke ferie well of her. and her shance to be Mr Burgomaster, an ples cod her will, will let her be shefe Shergeant?

Nip. Tush make no question of it. but sirra, if I need I must have one readie at call and commaund.

Ta. Call and Commaund? her may be assured hee shall not find her unprovided of a prance gallant wench, cod be plesed and praysed for it.

Nip. well hereafter wee will consider of it. here comes your old Master Brecknock. (*Enter Brecknocke.*)

Breck. Ôh is hee gone, in good sooth, I was afraid hartely of this gentle Athenian. surely wee will take some course for this Clubb lawe. ô Mr Niphell god morrow to you, you are welcome. Tavie wee have stayed from the Court hall this houre for the Sergeants. Is it not a shame Mr Niphell that knaves, that are maineteined by our table shall give noe better attendance?

Tavy. Her as come as soone as her can.

Bre. No, I am now goeing out of my office, you never regard mee. but I'le speake a good word for you.

Nip. Nea, good Mr Burgomaster, be not offended with him, lay the blame upon mee, I had some reason to imploy him.

11 may MS. 'nay' 25 Master MS. 'Mr'

Brec. Nea, Mr Niphill, the matter is not great betwixt you and mee. goe sirra, runne for the rest of your fellowes.

Tav. Nay, her as fetch her with a poxe.

Bre. I am now rendring up of my office. I pray god hee that comes after mee, may performe the duetie no better then I have done, | god send you good p. 8
shipping this yeare. I thanke god I have passed the billowes of the sea, I leave my office.

Nip. I hope sir if it be bestowed upon mee; so to carry my selfe, that I will not onely follow your good proceedings, but also if it may be, goe before you in government.

Bre. I, I doubt not but you will. but how doe your good bedfellowe?

Nip. By my troth sir shee is troubled with the trembling of the tongue.

Brec. It pleaseth you to saye so sir. but I wonder theise knaves sargeants come not away. wee must be their men, and waite upon their honours, ôh here they come. your worships be welcome.

Sar. Small worships sir.

Brec. Come, come, where be the rest of our societie? mee thinks it is the finest sight to see us goe cheeke by gole togither. but Tavy, runne to Mr Spruce our Towne Clarke, stay here hee comes. Puffe presently Puffe fetch Mr Romford, tell me of such a dwarfe, I never sawe such a long fellow. God morrow Mr Spruce.

52 you MS. 'your' 66 me MS. 'him'

Spruce. Good morrow Gentlemen, when shall this our duety be performed to putt offe the pristine head?

Nipp. Putt offe, t'is pittie such a pretie head should off.

Spru. Tush, you misconceive mee.

Nip. No, no, my wife never mist conceyving in her life. (*Enter Cricket.*)

Cricket. And effaith, Loggerhead are you there, I would theise aples were balls of lead, that they might but brayne one of you. but take this as it is.

(*Cricket hitts Mr Burgomasters head with an aple.*)

Nip. Hô is there no officers? such wrong? some gentle Athenian, after him Sargeants, after him. (*The Sargeants runne after him, a noyse within*, hold, keepe, stopp.)

Nip. This is strange they will offer us this indignitie being in this showe.

Spr. They dare doe any thing they thinke to offer us any ronge.

Bre. I even now a litle Ape, as bigg as my boy Jacke strocke at mee with his Club, and I could not come within him for feare of his knife.

Spr. By our Ladie but wee must have some remedie against this Club law, but who was it?

Puffe. A litle Ape, I thinke as hie as my knee, hee tooke mee such a riprapp on the head and told mee t'was Club law, and away hee gott betwene my leggs, and gave mee such a pestilent fall.

Nip. Why, what a company of bobies were yee? could you not catch him?

Tavy. As take her lodging | and teare the gentle p. 9 Athenians keepe her there till her as not have her.

Brec. well let us away unles wee be troubled with more of them. why Puffe hast thou forgott thy selfe? call Mr Rumford (*Puffe goes.*) Mee thinks this Burgomastershipp sitts heavier upon mee then my head upon my shoulders. Come letts begone, and fetch Mr Colbie and returne presently.

Puff. Mr Rumford comes sir, he'le meete you at Mr Colbies house.

Breck. well.

ACTUS 1us. Scena 5^{a}.

Enter Cricket.

Crick. Are yee gone? god speed you well. ôh [if] the welsh Rogue would have but followed mee into the hall, that wee might but had the villaine to the pumpe, wee would have given him skulls punishment effaith. ô Lord that I could but save mee as much money, as would buy mee a Scottish dagger to pricke the villaines. I have a huge great Dictionarie as bigg as my selfe almost, Il'e sell that, and buy mee a dagger. It shall be even so. I would I durst I faith, I could find in my heart but for my Tutor. Theise Tutors are such troublesome things. By the masse, hee hath

117 as much MS. 'as' ('much' written in the margin).

one, Ile steale that and save the money. But here comes gravities, I'le give them the cringe. (*Enter Philenius and Musonius.*)

Phi. But Musonius didst thou heare it of a certeintie?

Muso. make no question of it. see this litle villaine; twentie to one, but hee hath committed some good jeast or other.

Cric. Ô Mr Philenius how doe you, Mr Musonius how fares your bodie?

Phi. you litle Rakehell, how chanceth it you are not at your study?

Muso. Thou wantest but a litle brechinge.

Cric. Good Lord breeching, nothing but breching and studie. why they are the two worst things in the world. meethinks it is the Childest thinge to be breched, so schooleboylike, as for the other, it is not so good as they saye it is.

Muso. well Sirra, what busines have you heere?

Phi. Some Rakelly tricke or other.

Cric. Ô Lord Sir no, but a litle mirth with the sir reverence of the towne. I'le tell you Sirs Mr Brecknock the Chandler, the Burgomaster I meane, and I have had a full meete, but I got the wall of him, and hee came to catch mee, but I was for him, but even now if you had seene what a race wee had.

Phi. A race, may I entreate you upon what occasion?

Cric. Ô Lord Sir, the Aplewench used mee very

138 the MS. 'the the'

hardly, and I in a choller (as | men are subject unto passions) hurld them away and by good fortune hitt Mr Burgomaster on the head, after came the Sergeants, away goe I, there was hold, stopp, keepe, here, there, but I out ran the fatt Sargeant at a playne race, and turned short againe and gave him such a knocke, that I brake his head the dayntelest, that you could not chowse but laugh. p. 10

Muso. well sirra you are a wagg.

Phi. you must come over.

Cric. Come over againe, ô god that I were but as you are, I would have it better with theise Clownes.

Mus. Clownes sir boy.

Crick. I, Clownes, nea if wee have breching, studye, comming over againe, Sir boy, Ile leave you. the world will never be better, so long as such stayed gravities have any thing to doe, wee can doe nothing for them, but Il'e about more knaveries, Il'e persecute them.

(*Exit Cricket.*)

Phi. ffaith musonius this boy hath a good nimble witt, do'st thou not see how hee is moved with theise things, whereof wee seeme carelesse. why could a man behould such a rable of Loggerheads with patience?

Mus. Why Philenius theise are fitter to move pittie then procure patience, to see a heard of Asses, thinking themselves a troupe of sages, I would never wish a better object to my sences then theise.

Phi. why, but canst thou be well pleased to see

170 persecute See note on 2382.

such sepulchers the Image of divine authoritie, and them governe others which can scarcely mannage their owne affaires?

Muso. As well as see Venus shrine presented with base mould. when there is sufficient matter wanting, you must accept that which is most proporcionable to perfeccion.

Phi. I durst have sworne that this place where the muses be so conversant and the good Arts so nourished could not have byn so voyd of humanitie. I thought it unpossible that ignorance should have nestled where knowledg is so powerfull. but now I see my conjecture falsified. for if I should point out the true visage of Clownerie, I would accept of this for a true Idea.

Muso. ffaith to speake truely thou maist goe further and speed worse. Minerva our foundresse in my conceit was very provident in adjoyning herselfe to such druggs, how else should wee have them serviceable?

p. 11 *Phi.* Thou seest experience | hath shewed the contrarie, in stead of our servants they seeme to be our masters, their power is too absolute, they muddy slaves [thinke them selves] to good to be our servants.

Muso. I, and will retaine that thought, except some true spirited Gent[lemen] make them feele our stripes for their disobedience, and renewe the ancient Clublawe. had I but authoritie, I would curbe their foming mouthes, and shewe them by nature to be mere drudges.

Phi. Alas poore yonge brayne what couldest thou

208 mere MS. 'more'

effect more then those who have managed their actions by experience, and have had wisdome written in the furrowes of their face?

Muso. Experience hath made them too wise, but sirra shall wee bestowe some time to bringe them to their ancient duetie? I durst presume to effect it.

Phi. I, you may presume, yet you will hardly assume any thing by this presumption. But Musonius, I will follow thee, I am at thy service.

Muso. Now is the time of their Eleccion, when they will be plotting some villanie against us. I durst lay my head, the Bakerlie, lecherous, petifogging Niphle will be chosen Burgomaster, hee hath bought him a satten sute all readie, hee must have a fling at us, now if wee could but be partakers of their Counsell they were our owne.

Phi. why, that is easie, if wee could but humore their wives, they are such good kind loving gossips, that all theirs is ours, I knowe they will not conceale their owne thoughts much lesse their husbands seecrets, either this way wee must worke, or else be ignorant.

Muso. ffaith Philenius thy Counsell is allowable, but mens Censurs will passe hardly upon us for conversing with such unconstant gossips.

Phi. Never regard their Conjectures, but our owne intents. Lead on, Ile followe you.

ffinis Act 1. Scen. 5.

217 hardly MS. 'harly'

ACT 1us. SCENA 6ta.

Enter Brecknock, Romford, Colbie, Spruce; Tavie bringing out Cushions, and a table, Puffe, Catch, Niphle, the Electors, and Cipher.

Catch. Prethee Puffe keepe thy rancke.

Puff. you will teach mee will you? By my ffathers soull bell…

Breck. why how sauce boxes? If you be not more orderly I'le send you where you shall. Come, come my bretheren, letts about this geare, that I may be unloaded of this burthen. Mr Towne Clarke see that p. 12 all | the Electors be present, call their names.

Spruce. Mr Sixpenny, Mr Littleworth.

Breck. ffyne them.

Spr. Mr Halfecake, Goodman Cowby.

Cow. Here sir.

Spru. Mr Assely.

Cow. Ant please your worships my Landlord is gone to see his willowes lopt, h'ele be here by and by.

Brec. The Court must not stay for him, fine him, fine him, call the rest.

Spruce. Mr Lobson, Goodman Ketlebasen.

Ketl. Here sir.

Spru. Mr Thirtens.

Ketl. Ant please your worships, my gossip Thirtens went on wednesday to Thebes to buy some ffells at the leather fayre.

242 Prethee MS. 'Prether'

Brec. marry even fine Mr Thirtenes, a marke, that is, a groate more then his name. (*The Electors laugh at Mr Burgomasters jest.*)

Spruce. Mr Moone the elder.

Moone. I thought within this fourtenenight I should never have seene your worships againe, a scurvie Jade gave mee such a fall. (*Mr Moone is sicke and hath a kercher.*)

Spruce. Mr Silverburrowe.

Brec. Is hee not here? w'ele make him borrow silver or gold to pay his mercement. (*They laugh.*)

Spru. Mr Esdras, Mr ffescu, Mr Mallice.

Brec. Lett them be well fined, it is a shame for them.

Spru. Goodman Hornesbie.

Horn. Here sir. (*Brecknock neeseth.*)

(*Goosturd. Munne. Hornesby.* God blesse your worship.)

Spru. Mr South Cocks.

Ketl. There is none such sir.

Brec. It's Mr Westcocks, goodman Woodcocke. (*They laugh.*)

Spru. Mr Westcocks.

Ciph. it is so indeed.

Ketle. Hee keepes house in the Countrie, for I thinke hee hath left the Towne.

Brec. Hee was never otherwiselike.

Spru. Goodman Goosturde.

Goose. Here sir.

Brec. well said Oliver Goosturd, faith thou art a true-penny ever.

Goost. And please god sir Il'e performe my Christian duety, as long as I live.

Spru. Mr Jonas.

Cow. He was here even now. Goodman Tavie, is he not att your house?

Tavie. Her as truncke tere in te morning, he said ant please cod, her would call you goodman Cowper.

Spru. Goodman Nixon.

Breck. Nicke him oth' score. (*They laugh.*)

Spru. Goodman Cooperburne.

Gost. I sawe him hereabout, goodman Cowper, did you not see goodman Cooperburne?

Coop. Here sir.

Goost. Come, come, you have byn thrice called here, heres goodman Cooperburne sir.

Coop. Here sir, my wife was sicke and sent for mee sir.

Breck. The Court must neither staye for you nor your wife, the Duke must be served, well take off his fine, if hee were fined, for this once.

Spru. Mr Anderton.

p. 13 *And.* Here sir.

Spruce. Mr Slugg.

Ander. Mr Slugg why doe you [not] answere when you are called?

Slug. Here sir.

Breck. you have not your name for nothing, mee thinks you are very slowe. (*They laugh.*)

Spruce. Goodman Gallant, Goodman Tongue it.

Breck. This is gallant, that no man will tongue it, but wee cannot staye all the day on them. (*They laugh.*) Let us goe to it with those that wee have. Now Mr Towne Clarke certifie the cause.

Spruce. I will declare it presently. In the antient Persian Common-wealth, you shall finde very often, that the weale publike flourished in the time of the monarchy: Even so I say here, if I may be so bold to compare, comparisons being so odious, bringing in dissentions, hatred and mallice being so great enemies to a Common-wealth, and also—

Rumf. Nea, Mr Spruce leave theise circumprances, and come to the prologue of the matter.

Spruce. But I will hasten, for time hath winges. I cannot deny, but wee admired, that theise gentle Athenians dare compare, with us polititians, Machivillians; good St Mary what have they but wee have; they their Rector wee our Burgomaster, they their nurceries wee our fraternities, they their Philarches, wee our Bayliffs, they their anteambulers, we our Sargeants, they their nomenclators, wee our Cryers, they their Orator, et vos habetis me Henricum Spruce.

Brec. Truely Mr Spruce, you have parbraked your minde very well, now sir, for the cause of this zemblance.

Spruce. I will dispatch. The anchestors of this towne very well seeing the disconveniences which

342 Rector MS. 'Rectors' 343 Philarches MS. 'Philarche'

might arise by the continuance of magistrats, enacted and ordeyned, that our Burgomastership should be annuall, either thereby to pull downe them, that grewe prowd, or to ease them that laboured for the mayntenance of our estate; And to unload Mr Brecknock of his great paynes, which hee hath undergone for the common good, wee must discharge him of his office, and chuse some other of an upright conversation and integritie to be head over this our body.

Breck. I pray you doe, Il'e but speak a word or two, and discharg you of your dueties. you knowe it is an old adverb, so many men, so many meanings; p. 14 how then should I being but a | man please all, no indeed, I have not sought to please all, but in my Conscience to performe the duetie of a good magistrate, and though I say it that should not saye it, seldome comes the better. As every paire of stocks hath his appointed holes, some for great knaves, some for lesse; so is it in our Burgomastership: a man must have holes, that is, eares to heare their suites, some bigg eares, some great eares for great matters, some small eares for litle matters. Now seeing it is so (good fellowes of our incorporacion) if at any time my eare hath byn stopped, (as I am sure it hath not byn, but upon some great neede) I aske forgivnes, and crave pardon. If the gridiron be not scoured, the fish boyling thereon will sticke on, and so be broken into mammocks: so if the Governour be not scoured with the sand of sinceritie, the fish, that is to say, the Commonwealth will sticke unto it, and be utterly confiscated.

I hope there is not any can or will say, that I have consumed or broken any thing, god is my Judge, I have not (*hee is non plus*).

Cipher. no truely.

Breck. neither would I, that worthy man—(*non plus againe*). (*Goosturd laugheth.*)

Breck. How now Goosturd? you goosecape you. why sirra not know hoe I am?

Goost. In truth sir, I did not laugh.

Brec. I will make you knowe, that I represent the person of the Duke.

Goost. Truly, sir I did not laugh.

Breck. No, no, goe you and stand here a while. come hether, I meane you Mr Moone, did you not heare him laugh?

Moone. Ant please your worship by Cocke, I did not heare him laugh.

Breck. Stand you by there; come hither goodman Cowper, I am sure, you will tell mee truth, goe too and saye

Cowp. Indeed sir, I can say no—

Breck. Goe to, to it.

Cowp. I can say nothing to it.

Brec. Can you not so sirra? well, sett ffive pounds on his head.

Spru. Is your name Thomas Cowper?

Cowp. I am not ashamed of my name, my name is Roger Cowper.

Breck. Are yee all of a packe? Il'e take a round Course with you all.

Cowp. Nea, I pray you sir, I thinke—

Breck. Goe to.

Cowp. I thinke [he] did smile, but I know not well.

Breck. well then stand you there. come hither
p. 15 sirra, goodman Cowper is an | honest man, hee hath told mee the truth, goe to confesse if you will have any favour.

Rumf. Ay, Ay, dea, dea, Oliver Goosturd it will make the matter better for you effaith.

Goost. Indeed Mr Rumford to tell your worships true, seeing I must needes tell, I did laugh, but sir reverence to you and to the bench, it was because goodman Cowper made a scape.

Ciph. Nea, you must not thinke you could scape Mr Burgomasters hands, I tell you hee is the wisest governour in his goverment that came this 20. yeares, hee will ferrit you the truth.

Breck. Nea, I thanke god Mr Cipher, I have examined harder matters then theise, and have found out the truth. Go your wayes now, and behave your selves better hereafter. take off their ffines, but now to proceed—Over and besides there be some evill disposed persons who have called mee cruell man. Indeede, I must confesse I am something angry by nature and once I made a foule fault by fettering a wench to keepe her from her bawderie; besides that I knowe nothinge, whereby I may be blamed. Now therfore it [is] your dueties (to you Mr Electors I speake it) to chuse some man like unto mee, who may followe my stepps and with a good courage preserve our ancient liberties, which hoping you will doe, as I received this dignitie at your hands: so I render it againe into your fingers. Now therfore Mr Electors you were best about your dueties. This therefore is the cause of our dissemblance, and the whole fect of the matter.

Spru. ffor your care and studie of the publike good wee are much bound to you good Mr Brecknocke and suppose your carriage to be soe good, that no man justly can finde fault with it.

Rumf. And you are of my mynd, for you have performed your duetie verie deftlye.

Colby. I, I, Ile warrant you, he that sayes hee will doe better, may doe worse.

Breck. ffaith Mr Rumford, who shall be Mr Burgomaster now?

Rumf. By my soule, Mr Shavett, hee is a very honest man, hee is worth twa hundred poundes.

Colbie. And hee will undoe us all as a man should undoe an Oyster, hee loves the gentle Athenians too well, the other you know | his father was Baker, hee p. 16
brought him up pretelie to his booke, hee is a pretie pettifogging Lawyer a kinde of Attorney, hel'e drawe bloud of theise gentle Athenians, he'le tickle them effaith. (*The Electors crie within* A Niphill, A Niphill.)

Spruce. God hath blessed us in giving us such a Burgomaster.

Tavy. Cots plude her ferry clad her arships Burgomaster.

Breck. yea, I told you it would be hee. effaith, hee is worthy of it, is hee gone for?

Tavy. Her will come pie and pie.

Rumf. Nea, I doubt not, but he'le dea very well.

Breck. Loe here hee comes. Mr Towne Clarke certifie, informe.

Spru. Renowned Mr Niphle, knowing by the good carriage of your selfe in sundrie affaires, that you are man fitt to beare rule, wee have errected and constituted you the pilott of this our shipp, which you must not refuse, but receive with great alacritie and courage.

Niphle. Although my sondry imployments in greater affayres, and my late sicknes might sufficiently excuse mee; yet pittying this ruinous estate, I will not refuse it, but receive it, that I may renue it, and make it, a flourishing Cittie.

Colbye. It were great pittie you should.

Rumf. marry the towne wade have micke want of you.

Niph. Now therfore being your Governour, marke how I informe you the waye of obedience. Marcus Aurelius that famous Roman English Orator saith, old men for witt, and yong men for wisedome, I would say yong men for old men and old men for yonge men, but I will assure you that it is a wise speech; The same Aurelius thinketh it impossible for a man to be a Bayliffe, Headsman, Constable or muchomar, that is timbersome or afraid, which being true, as it is no lye, let us fetch an example from our selves; to what a lowe estate have wee byn brought by too much

477 Niphle MS. 'Niple' 482 *Niphle* MS. 'Niphe'
497 muchomar Query 'wacheman'

timerousnes of former magistrats so that wee have byn made servants of Rulers, I could not but admire that men in | authoritie should be so base minded. p. 17
Did wee not see a snipp snapp Barber give the most worshippfull of our societie (the Bakerly knave)? I, and had not a yonge lustie ladd taken it in hand it had byn pocketted up to our great discredit. I say and will stand to it wee have had but meane Rulers of our Cittie very fooles.

Cip. Doe you meane mee Sir?

Niph. Peace Cipher peace, they were not able to governe their owne private families, but now I hope you have chosen one, that shall renewe the ancient credit and make them stoupe, that spurne at our Authoritie, neither will cut the throate of iniquitie like a Calfe, nor knocke downe sinne like a bullocke, but I will so boult the meale of this Cittie, that I will make it all fyne flower, and the rest I will make into horsbreade, and turne it into the manger of distruccion; and as for theise gentle Athenians, I will rout out the whole generacion of them, and make the vagabonds seeke their dwellings, they shall not nestle with us in our streets, nor out brave us in our owne dunghills, they shall trudg, they shall trudge, if Nicholas Niphle be head of this Citie, they shall packe with bag and baggage. But impaciencie maks mee forgett my selfe. Now therfore seeing I am your governour you shall

505 knave)? Is the sentence incomplete or do the bracketed words form the object to 'give'?

515 will Query 'will I' 524 Niphle MS. 'Niple'

be obedient servants, and assist mee with life and goods to be at my commaundement, else I will not manure theise affaires. sai, will yee?

All. wee will, wee will.

Niphl. If you will not, I my selfe now I have power will punish those stifnecked students, and shewe that I have to commaund, therfore yee performe your duetie.

Spruce. you may presume upon the good endevours of the Cittisens. else sir, you may use your owne discretion.

Rumf. you may put them to micke swinke else.

Breck. Hy, hy, it is hy noone.

Ciph. It is indeede.

Colby. Truly my stomake tell mee so.

Niph. Now sirs seeing you have performed your duetie, I indite you to a feast; now then lett goe in, p. 18 followe mee till the feast bee | solempnized, which being finished wee must bee here againe presently to consult about sundry affaires. Tavie, take thy place next my person.

All. God give you joye Mr Burgomaster, god give you joye.

Niph. I thanke you good subjects all, god blesse you good subjects all. I thanke you good subjects all.

ACTUS 1us. SCENA 7a.

Enter Cricket. Catch. Tavie.

Cric. Subjects, this arrogant asse thinks himselfe some litle king, hee carries his nose up in the winde

532 *Niphl.* MS. 'Nipl.' 543 indite Query 'invite' lett Query 'letts'

and doth snuffe it like some Brewers horse. the asse must needes imitate absurditie; you would not thinke how it greeves mee, that theise blocks should feast it so quietly, and yet the spite is, I cannot invent how to disturbe them, but that welsh Rogue troubles mee for following mee so hard, well Ile cousen him of his dinner, if I helpe him to something else: Ile goe to him boldly, for I am sure hee knowes mee [not], hee inquired my name, but nobody would tell it him; and besides I have disguised my selfe a litle, faith whither hee knowes mee or not Ile venture it, thats certeine. but I wonder how a murren a welshman should come to Athens, but I thinke in my conscience, there came but one in a shipp, and he was the one came hither. well now Ile about my trickes, tic, tac, toc. I pray sir is not Tavie within?

Catch. I, hee is within.

Crick. may a man speake with him?

Catch. I cannot tell, hee is busie, but Ile see; ho Tavie.

Tavie. Ho call her.

Catch. Here is one would speake with you.

Tavy. what a poxe is her, can her tell?

Catch. A gentle Athenian.

Tavy. what will her have some fittle? Cot be thanked here is some good pastie and pie.

Catch. Come see.

Tavy. God morrow to her, will her speake with mee?

Crick. I good Mr Tavie, I am so bold as to trouble you honest Mr Tavie.

Tavy. will her tell mee why?

Crick. marry sir, a Gentleman one Mr Morgan, that is new come to towne is very desirous to speake with you a worde or two, good Mr Tavie, honest Mr Tavie.

Tavie. Nea, cover her head man, Cods plud man cover her head, why the pox is that arships Gent[leman] come to towne to speake to her? fere shall her speake |
p. 19 with her arships?

Crick. Att our lodging, followe mee and Ile bring you to him instantlie.

Tavy. nea her must serve Mr Burgomaster arship first, tell her, her will come anone.

Crick. Nea, if you come not presently her must take horse, and begone, her stay upon you, therfore honest Mr Tavie, if you will follow mee doe, if not I have done my Arrand.

Tavie. Holt what saucie Jacke prat a pox on her, her will goe, but her will come home againe presently.

Crick. As you will for that, I pray you letts make hast.

Tavie. will her trincke man?

Crick. No, no, tis too, too grosse, letts be gone.

Tavie. I, I, leade the way, tell her how her wellcome.

Crick. Ile lead you where you shall be safe theise two houres.

finis Act 1. Scen. 7^{mae}.

612 7^{mae} MS. '7^{mi}'

ACTUS 1us. SCENA 8va.

Enter Puff. Mounsier.

Puff. Theise sweating......are halfe drunken alreadie, Ile goe see if I can meete with any boone Companions, that I may shewe them what good cheere our towne makes. me thinks our new Burgomaster begins to laye it on lustely. ô that I could meete with any of my fellowe Puffers. Let mee see, there is a certeine ffrenchman called Mounsier grand Combatant. I was in his company the other day, it would make a horse laugh to heare him talke. If I can mete him Ile carrie him to the feast, as rounde as a Julers boxe, he is as good as a foole to make us sport: gods daggers, here he is, he shall goe with mee thats certeine.

Mouns. By cod me cannot stay in de house, me cannot tell de reason, all de good fellowes be gone, I se come in de towne verie be merie.

Puff. O Mounsier, I am verie glad I have mett with you, effaith you shall stay.

Mouns. ô Mr Puff in trot, me verie clad to see your worship, come sall wee goe trincke a quart of wyne at de cape?

Puff. Staye you shall goe with mee.

Mouns. Sall wee goe prede weder? in de Cape?

Puffe. No, here. Mr Burgomaster makes a great feast, you shall goe with mee to dinner. |

629 verie Query 'vill', the error being due to 'verie' below.

p. 20 *Mouns.* To dinner? Mr Burgomaster make good shere, is good wine?

Puff. I, come letts goe.

Mouns. ô Lord sir, tis no madder for dat, mee taunke you for your courtesie. I intrant I will follow you.

Puff. You shall be verie welcome.

Mouns. me taunke you.

ACTUS 2^{dus}. SCENA 1^{a}.

Mounsier solus.

Mouns. Intraunt, Intraunt is no good shere, de scurvy fleshmakers, feefe, all te flesh, all ale, all Beere, is scurvie dinner, ne vine, de scurvie Rogue Puffe make good Cordileere, abuse mee, he spake ffrench, de great clowne so laugh, abuse, all so full Cowe, mutton, velt, porridg, is not tart, not custart, ne vine ne tinge Cavelero intraunt, wee will goe the Accademick's, wee will be merry, is better goods fellowes there.

ACTUS 2us. SCENA 2^{a}.

Niphil, Colbie, Rumford, Cipher, Brecknock, Sargeants, Electors doe their dueties to Master Burgomaster, and goe out.

Niph. Surely it could not be but avayleable, if you durst undertake it Mr Colbie.

644 you MS. 'your'

Colby. Before god sir, it would make them disburse their Coine, and wee might be honest savers by it, but let every man give me his Counsell.

Niph. You say well. Mr Brecknock, I commaund you to mount your judgment how wee might bring under theise, as wee call them, gentle Athenians, who being proud in regard of a Goddish called Mineva call us falsly hoyden Athenians, whereas indeed they themselves are but our vassalls, are they not called Ragge tayles, longe tayles, tatter tayles, wee Burgomaster, Hedsmen, which signifieth no lesse then [our] worthinesse and theire basenes, which shewes us to be the head, they the tayles, I say, how wee might make them yeld true allegiance to their sovereigne, whereas now they seeke to bring us under them, or at the | least to p. 21 make us one with them and so be our servants.

Breck. By my tricks in my foolish opinion, Ile tell you what; wee have a great many of prettie smugg girles in the towne, they shall gett the gentle Athenians in, and they shall gett them with child, and all the gentle Athenians shall have basterds and then the gentle Athenians shall be married and so wee shall be ridd of them.

Ciph. This cannot but be availeable.

Rumf. The poore snakes are not able to keepe theire barnes, what a deale shall wee doe with them ?

Breck. ffoh, wele make them our bondslaves or any thinge.

Ciph. I, any thing, any thinge.

678 they MS. 'the' 681 prettie MS. 'pettie'

Niph. I wonder men of your place will bringe forth such reasons, what say you Mr Colbye?

Colby. ffaith, if wee could but gett away theire gilded staves they would not jett it as they doe, Ile tell you, wele say they be full of rich pearles, and soe they shall be broken for the Duke and wee will feast upon them.

Niph. Ha, ha, ha, to to bad, so wee shall be found lyers, and repaire them againe. what say you Mr Rumford?

Rumf. Mary sir twere very good to twacke their Crags and make their bones sore.

Ciph. I could saye some thinge, but it is no matter, I know what I know.

Spruce. I thinke it were verie good to putt up a supplicacion togither with the informacions of the injurie they have offered us and so to crave constraint of their liberties.

Niph. what say you to fire their lodging?

Breck. nea, good sir take heed what you doe, my house is not farre of, I had rather spend 20. and 10. nobles, two.

Niph. I tell you in a common good the firing of one private house is not to be respected, but I will not doe it. now every man marke my charge and take my commaundement, you Mr Colebie shall forestall the markett and carrie away their Corne for you have obteyned your suite.

Rumf. what the deale shall I doe?

713 20. Query '20. pounds'

Niph. you Mr Rumford shall see them receive their reward, I say by some manner of meanes to have them well beaten.

Rumf. Iffaith, Ile lay on their sides, they shall have their owne Clublawe.

Niph. Mr Brecknock Mr Cipher and the rest shall be my assistants, and you Mr Spruce shall drawe the Articles, doe it presently, doe it I saye, tis your duetie.

Spruce. I pray you sir, let every one give his Article and Ile forme | them. p. 22

Niph. They shall: beginne Mr Brecknocke.

Breck. what if I put up this, that the gentle Athenians spend more upon ffidlers under the colour of musitions in rowing downe the river then would mainteine Mr Burgomasters house and the 3. Sargeants very sufficiently.

Niph. Hold your hand Mr Spruce, hold, me thinke you might have more witt, then to write such a foolish Article, they would say wee were very fooles, if they sawe this. Mr Rumford yours.

Rumf. That the lads spend more in shoetyings then 60. headsmen doe in scarlet. why wadd not an end of a point, or a pece of a glove serve but they must spend a tester, I say sixe pence, upon Ribans?

Niph. note downe that, it will informe their prodigalitie, I thanke you good Mr Rumford.

Rumf. Nea faith, it is not so mickle worth.

Niph. Mr Colby yours.

Colby. That whereas it is enacted and ordeyned,

736 Burgomasters MS. 'Burgomaster'

good Mr Spruce, write in the yeare 1400. they contrarie to the same act, have violentlie carried away and them used sending them home diseased with tympanies, so that they and theirs lye upon our hand to our great charge and impovishment.

Niph. This will serve, Mr Cipher yours.

Ciph. what you please, Sir, that shall be, god hath given you the gift of speaking.

Niph. And you of silence. Now Masters letts heare the supplication.

Spruce. The worthy Burgomaster, and injured men of this incorporacion being overladen with the burthen of injuries doe prostrate themselves at your feete, craving your aide and assistance against the unsupportable ronges of the gentle Athenians. And least that you should thinke, that causlesse wee complaine, wee have here sett downe the causes of our griefe, which hoping you will redresse, thus wee article.

Niph. what is the first?

Spruce. The worthy Burgomaster &c.

Niph. Sett it downe the thrice worthy Burgomaster, the rightworshippfull Mr Nicholas Niphle. it may be they will heare it the sooner for my sake. So Mr Spruce see theise dispatched, well wele come on them everie waie, by force, by complaint. if my conjecture faile me not, wee shall have the day. My Masters looke to your charges, and performe the duetie of good subjects, wee must now depart for I have detayned you somewhat longe.

752 carried away Query 'carried away the daughters of our townsmen'
755 impovishment Query 'impoverishment'

Rumf. Ile bange them; and I doe not, the deale on my cragge.

Ciph. And whatsoever youle say or doe Mr Burgomaster Ile say it is well done. |

Niph. And in so doeing you shall shewe your selves p. 23
good townsemen, but lett us be gone. where are Seargeants? wheres Tavie? fore god I wonder I sawe him not at the feast, doth he waite on him selfe? let us be gone.

ACTUS 2us. Scena 3^{a}.

Tavie solus.

Tavy. All the deeles in hell take her, what the poxe is her all gone? plutter her nayles, her was never served such a pranke in all her life. A litle knave made her loose her dynner, and her packe peaten, and her bellie is emptie. Cotts plutt, her was not care two rushes for the Clerigalls, as for her pastie, ôh her pastie and her pye, and pest tart. But marke her now, shall tell her tale, a ferry satt tale, which makes her eyes to water, and her heart to weepe. Tavy a shiefe Sergeant, dell in the mountaines, spend all her dayes, was goe see Mr Morgan her Countryman, in the Accademie, ant Tavie was followe a litle knave, up his Chamber. when Tavye was tere, Tavie was locked up, was not lett out, Tavie staied tere all tynner and was verie cold, but a litle knave was steale, so gallant Tavie was wipped ant abusd ant loose her tynner, tell her was not [tat] a ferie coode sat tale, was verie true. and now loose all cood shere and loose Mr Burgomasters cood will. her will have some of her plute and revenge. But now her will goe to Mr Burgomaster and tell her tale, and please cod, and scuse her selfe. *Exit.*

ACTUS 2us. SCENA 4^{a}.

Mistrisse Colbie sola.

Mris Colbie. Jesus blesse me, what doe our men meane to abuse such proper Gentlemen, such learned men, that conjure the devill into a Circle and put him againe in hell, and doe such strang things as they be? In faith they themselves are such hoydens, that they cannot endure such muske companions. In good truth there was one at our house the other daye, neere trust mee, if he did me not good at the heart to looke upon him, I offered him but a cup of beere, and god is my Judge, my husband told mee I would bestowe all that
p. 24 I had upon him, Ile lay my life | the Cuckold is jealous, but Ile cry quit with him. Good Lord that I could meete with that same good Gentleman Mr Musonius, if I would not tell him all my husbands knaveries I pray god I never have good of him, but good lord, here comes Mris Nifle harken what shee sayes. (*Enter Mris Nifle.*)

Mris Nifle. I faith, I faith, is it even so? I dare pawne my maidenhead hee is goeing about to cut queane me, he hath had so much private conference with Tavie. all must be gone forsooth, great matters no doubt with that welsh raskall. Good lord, I cannot but wonder, why other women should please him better then my selfe. I am sure I am not so foule, I confesse I am none of the fairest, and yet effaith some have counted me none of the brownest, if I were it were something, but I thanke god I am as proper as some of them, it is a marvell he is so lustie abroade and quiet at home. But goe you abroad, and if I be not quit with you, never let me be Mris Nifle more, Ile make the gentle Athenians, whom yee hate so much, as far in as your selfe, if they [be] not too modest. Ile have a sonne this yeare a Gentleman, effaith, I will. but yonder is Mris Coleby, Ile see if shee be not in my taking.

Mris Colby. Ile goe to her, deaven Mris Nifle, how doth Mr Burgomaster, and all at home forsooth? all well forsooth I hope.

Mris Nifle. God lord, what doe you meane to inquire after Mr Burgomaster? twentie to one, it is you that doth cut-queane mee.

Mris Col. ffaith so merily disposd, marie you are happy, that can be cuckqueand, Ile warrant you, I shall never take myne in that fault.

Mris Nifle. By my maidenhead you'r in a miserable case. But whether are you walking?

Mris Colby. nay, mistrisse Nifle thats counsell.

Mris Nifle. Good Lord ladie, are you so squeamish as though I know you not, indeede you are a wanton, nere trust me, if you be not, but if it be so as you saye, I cannot blame you.

840 a MS. 'no'

Mris Colbie. It is even as I tell you, but how should I helpe my selfe now?

Mris Nifle. why let others; among such a companie of Gallants, I would nere want one.

Mris Col. why, but theise gentle Athenians are such maiden fac't fellowes, ne're credit me, if I did not p. 25 carrie Mr Musonius up into my bedchamber | and shewed him my bed and arras hanging, and shutt the doore, and asked him if it were not a faire and soft bed and yet the foole understood mee not, and therupon I fell of talking of fyne lynnen, and therupon I had him see if my smocke was not fyne holland, and yet the foole understood mee not. what could have a woman done more? Unlesse—

Mris Nifle. And so I warrent you hele be bold enough, if you serve him such an other tricke.

Mris Col. But here hee comes and Mr Philenius with him, they two are great and why not wee two?

ACTUS 2^{s}. SCENA 5^{a}.

Musonius, Philenius, Mistris Colbie Mris Nifle.

Muso. See, Philenius, here are our gossips, now wee have good opportunitie to worke them.

Phi. I, I, good warrent you, let us give them the unset, Gentlewomen god save you.

Mris Nifle. Mr Philenius how does your bodie?

Mris Col. Good lord Mr Musonius, what a stranger

882 *Musonius* MS. 'Musunius'

are you at our house ? doe you thinke that there are beares at our house ?

Muso. No, Mris Colbie, but fearefull least in this suspitious age I should give any occasion of scandall to theise quick tongues.

Mris Nifle. Good Lord Mr Philenius how cold you are ! you spoile your selfe with too many bookes, why myne eyes would out if I should read halfe so much.

Phile. I, your eies are ordeyned for other uses, my Eies have vowed themselves to theise studies. I but why were you two togither ?

Mris Niph. marry we were talking of your unkindnesses.

Mris Colbie. By my honestie, we said you were verie Churles.

Muso. why doe you impose such a hard sentence upon us ?

Phile. Our natures are opposite to such.

Mris Niph. I know not, but I wonder you are so squeamish, that upon great curtesies and proffers, you give not the common curtesie, so much as a kisse.

Phile. A kisse. why theise are the common curtesies of sleight lovers, we deeme kisses but trifles, our loves are placed in our inward hart.

Mris Col. I pray you lett mee | have a trifle. p. 26

Muso. This is too sleight a demaund fitting thy conceit. but how can wee affect you, when those that are neere unto [you] prosecute us with such [unkindness]? I meane your husbands.

Mris Niph. By my troth you say true, but god knowes it is not our faults, wee wish it otherwise.

Mris Colbie. yea and you would but looke on us and like us and love us now and then, that ther might be some familiaritie betwene us, I knowe what I would doe.

Musonius. As farre as any Civilitie will permitt, wee are att your service, but what would you doe?

Mris Colby. Marrie any whatsoever.

Phile. (*Aside.*) The more unconstant gill thou. but doe you assent unto her?

Mris Niphie. I beshrewe my hart els.

Muso. why then you knowe how irksome wee are to your husbands, and upon that they are alwayes plotting some villany against us. would you but informe us of their pretences, that wee might prevent them, you might gaine to yourselves eternall lovers.

Mris Nifle. wee will doe it, so you be men of your words.

Mris Colbie. In faith wee will doe it. but we must not have you to modest, and to beginne to shewe you how we will keepe our promise, I tell you I heard all the men in our towne crying out against Clublawe, and said you had marred them, and they would be avenged of you and in the end determined to beate you with your owne weapons, and make you feele Clublawe.

932 upon that In the MS. a cross (+) is written over 'that' Query 'how that'

941 in our towne MS. 'in our towne (in our towne)'

944 your MS. 'you'

Muso. But when shall this be?

Mris Colbie. To morrow at a Cudgill play, all the yong lads in the towne will be upon you, therefore looke to your selves, I am sure I can doe no more.

Mris Nifle. Will you being Gentlemen be beaten downe by a company of Hoydens?

Phile. you cannot carry such a base conceit of us.

Muso. But as you have begune, so good mistris Colbie let us have further intelligence of it to morrow.

Mris Colbie. Tush Mris Colbie, I had rather you would call mee Besse Colbie, come you must leave this Mris and Mr, if you meane to be true friends.

Mris Niph. In troth Mris Colbie, it were enough to make our husbands jealous, | if they should see us p. 27 here, therefore Gentlemen we must crave pardon, if we can doe you no service.

Mris Colby. Gods bodikens you say true. my suger cakes will be over baked, Mr Musonius, you will looke to your promise, we will keepe ours.

Muson. Presume upon us.

Mris Nifle. I pray you Mris Colby let us tast of your sugar cakes.

Mris Colby. I pray you come good Mris Nifle, forsooth they be homely ones I warrant you. *Exeunt.*

Muson. Sirra Philenius, what an inticement were here to incontinencye, inough to corrupt the chastest thoughts, but let us not be carefull of our credits to neglect the common good. If we passe in some small actions, I hope welldisposed Judgments will ponder our intents.

Phile. ffirst for their husbands, lett us followe that, which they have begune, and use but their owne weapons, and turne them against themselves, but as for them lett us feede them with vaine delayes, least the Muses be not propitious unto us in our studies, being such profest enemies to Venus.

Muson. I assent to thee; and for mine owne parte, I hope my thoughts are of a higher pitch then to enter into such kennell thoughts, and dare almost promise for thee, but sirra, lett us goe certifie theise things to our freinds and see the performance of Clublawe.

Phile. Content, Ile busie my thoughts upon this Clownish subject, to bring it to effect. *Exeunt.*

ACTUS 2us. SCENA 6^{a}.

Cricket solus.

Crickett. Never trust mee, if I be not overjoyed to thinke how I fitted Mr friend Tavie, how finely he was last, what sweet red lashes he had on his shoulders. I never sawe a villaine take it more patiently, Ile warrent you, the villaine hath byn in as many Clerigalls in his life as I have gathered phrases, this is worth some mirth, p. 28 but I must be the man that must | make the Clownes yeald when all is done. I have it that will make them pay for it, but you thinke I am no man of my word,

980 profest In the MS. though the word is written in full, the 'p' has the turn which indicates 'pro'.

well be it so, but yet if you knewe all you would honour mee presently. I following the villaines and dogging them up and downe as it is a part of my study to play the Eivesdroper (as I can doe it pretily) at Mr Colebies parlour windowe there I heard such a sackfull of greasie consultations offensive to any good witt, there to be short I heard that Mr Colbie the Collier should convey away Corne under his coles to night. I away presently came hither consulting upon it how I might worke upon this villaine. what if I goe nowe in the dearth, and tell the poore people, that they plucke out the villaines eyes; no hange them, our authority shall make them stoupe. Ile even goe and tell Mr Musonius and Philenius of it, I am sure it is imprisoning at the least, they will hamper him in a paire of shackles or some thinge or other from our Rector. faith shall be even so. but what if they will not medle with it? why then Ile search them out some waye or other thats certeine, Ile about it. *Exit.*

finis Actus 2^{di}.

ACTUS 3us. Scena 1^{a}.

Crickett solus.

Crick. Ah you rascall Coleby you, if I be not on your skirts, if all hold, lett mee be putt into the blacke bill. By great chaunce I had noe sooner gone hence, but I presently mett with the two Gentlemen

1014 shall Query 'it shall'

who after I had certified them of it, you would not thinke what a company of good [fellows] they gave mee and presently they gott a writt (to attach him) from Mr Rector. Now sir, they them selves are watching in a friends house, and I am here verie well imployed, a scout to espy his comming and then certifie them of it and call them out ; so that they are but my p. 29 adjuvants, I am the cheife agent in this | matter. You shall see how gallantly we'le performe it. But let mee see, what time of night is it ? Yet it is not much past tenne of the clocke, and I warrent you it will be eleaven ere this Collierly Cornemonger come. what shall I stand here all this while like John Drome ? ffaith I shall sleepe, well I cannot, I must about some tricke or other. what let mee [see] my instruments. What a plague how came I by this rope ? ô now I knowe. surely, I will use this, but how ? what if I strangle the next fellowe that comes and gett on his backe and hange upon the rope ? I can doe it in a trice aswell as the best hangeman of them all. No I will not least I should crie guiltie before Mr Burgomaster, and he shall say, here I indite you by the name of Nic. Crickett. nowe I have founde it. so here Ile tye my rope and see what fortune will befall mee. ôh god could I but breake one of their necks I were a most happie man, let mee see, is my voice cleare ? hem, it will serve. murder, murder*, I am slaine, helpe, helpe Mr Burgomaster, helpe, murder, murder. * *A rope was tied at Mr Burgomasters dore.*

1026 good [fellows] In the MS. there is a gap after 'good'.

ACTUS 3us. Scena 2a.

Niphill. Tavy. Puff. Catch.

As they came out of the dore he tripps up theire heeles with a rope, and beates them with the Clubb.

Puff. ô good Lord, will yee murder mee ?

Crick. no Il'e not stay. (*he stepps aside.*)

Tavie. A poxe on her, Puff great knave almost breck her packe.

Catch. Nea, I am cleane spoiled, good Mr Burgomaster rise.

Niphle. This is strange, before god, a rope before my dore ? what a peece of knaverie is this ? looke about if you can see any of theise crackropes.

Tavie. A poxe on her, was take her heels.

Puff. Ile warrent you he is gone a good [mile] by this time.

Crick. not so farre but hee sees you.

Catch. I have hurt my legg shrodly.

Crick. I would thou | hadst broke thy necke. p. 30

Nifle. This is some tattertaild Athenian, but if I live Ile make them keepe their lodgings, they shall not goe about our streets at this time of the night.

Sargeant. Shall wee be gone sir, tis something late.

Niph. you may be gone, but Tavie stay.

Crick. nea, then Ile come a stepp neerer.

Sergeants. God give your worships good night.

1072 necke MS. 'necke necke'

Nifle. Now thou and I am here alone I neede not stand upon points.

Tavie. Na, ant her arship tell her of points and knacks and knaveries, ant her knowe her love flesh. but what is her will and desire?

Cricket. In faith Mr Burgomaster are you a muttonmonger? one stepp nyer.

Niph. ffaith Tavy, I was at thy house to day, and there I sawe the pretie wench, which thou toldst mee of before, I like her well, shee looks like a good holsome wench, and to be short, we magistrats are but men, and therefore followe Venerie, therefore Tavy I must use her, I tell thee in plaine termes, I must quench this naturall heate.

Crick. I would I had the quenching of it.

Tavie. But when will her come? her shall what her will.

Niph. ffaith honest Tavie, I cannot hold out long, lust grows on, therefore I prethe, see shee be readie against 12. of the Clocke, and then Ile come, but Tavie, be secrett, for if you lett a ragtaild Athenian knowe of it, you undoe us all.

Crick. ffie, no lett not them know it.

Tavy. Nea, and Tavie prate take her necke of, give her a wort, but how shall her knowe her from a knave.

Crick. I marrie, there is no such word in all the dictionarie.

1083 ant There seems to be some corruption here. Perhaps 'ant' has crept in from the line above.

1104 but Should 'but' be omitted or should it be made to precede 'give' above?

Niph. marrie well remembred, thus it shall be, Ile knocke thrice, and call Tavie, and then if I be hee, Ile say I burne.

Tavie. well then if her doe not say I purne, her must not lett her in.

Niph. no, in any case, Ile warrent thee Ile say soe.

Tavie. well her goe ant have her prideled and sadled against her arships come.

Niph. I doe, this lust torments mee, Ile goe in and disguise my selfe and come to the good girle presently. *Exit.*

Crick. Ô fortune thou favourest us, whatsoṁever wee doe some happie event or other presently ensues. And [is] it not you | mecanick slaves, who crie out p. 31 upon us for wenches and your selves such bawdie knaves? how I triumph in this, that wee may cry out of this lecherous villaine, and tell him of his holesome girle and of his burnings. If we can doe nothing els, wele fill all the Towne full of Rimes of him. wele paint all the Boggards with papers and so disgrace him, that wele make him hange him selfe. Ile goe tell Musonius of it presently. but stay, I beleive there comes my marke. I stand aside and heare my loger-pate.

ACTUS 3us. Scena 3a.

Enter Colbie prying about.

Cole. I thanke my starres heres all fallen out as I would have.

Crick. I, and as I would to.

Cole. And here is no creature stirring.

Crick. yet blinde Bayard, heres a beare will bite you.

Cole. Come, come on, good fellowes, all is passing well. (*the Coliars enter.*)

Crick. Ile goe to the Gentlemen presently to come and take them. (*Exit.*)

Colbie. Now afore god I cannot but laugh at theise vild Athenians, they count us simple, when they themselves are most foolish. here is a simple tricke I promise you. fill my sacks mouthes full of Coles, whereas theire bellies be stuft with corne. I marvell which of them could have invented such a thing.

1 *Colier.* Nea, if it come to invention, god helpe them, what have they in their lodgings that is good and necessarie but they have it from us? their larder house, their bakehouse, their kitchen, no not so much as their house of office in theire backsides, only they make theirs to differ from ours in name and in bignes.

2 *Collier.* well said fellow John, I perceive thou cariest some thing els besids burthens, I would have bene hanged, if any one of theise corner capp slaves in the towne could have made such a speech to so good purpose in a whole daye.

3 *Collier.* what a wondring keepes thou at him, as if his witt were not common to all of us. why I tell thee, the very name Porter signifies no lesse then

1162 common MS. 'com-' at end of line. The word is not completed.

wittie, doth any man | send a foole with a burthen, or an asse with an errand? p. 32

1 *Collier.* If hee doe lett him be sure to send the Cryer after him, or els goe seeke himselfe like a foole when he hath done.

2 *Coll.* Nea, I thanke god, I was never sent of an arrand. But I could doe it well enough, and returne home with out sending for.

3 *Collier.* Yett once fellow Dicke, doe not you remember how you accused a stone instead of a gentle Athenian, for tripping up your heeles and biting you by the buttockes when he had done?

Colbie. Marry you make my worship merrie, here be merrie fellowes indeede. how can a man chuse, but have his worke done, when he hath such a company of wittie fellowes about it? hold heres one groat more to Dicke fort, when he comes home for this, but I feare mee wee staie to long, the bargmen thinke wele never come. away take up the sackes and letts be gone.

Colliers. when you please sir, lead you the way and wele followe.

ACTUS 3us. Scena 4a.

Musonius. Philenius. Cricket and his company.

Crick. Here they be, make hast quickly, or els they will be gone.

Colbie. Alas wee are betrayed, make hast and shift for your selves.

Crick. Nea, help, help, I have one of them.

Muso. If that they will not yeild, downe with them.

Phile. Hoe Mr Colbie well mett, what busines have you to be abrode now?

Cole. why sir, about my busines to send a fewe coles downe by water, I hope sir, you can take no offence at it.

2 *Port.* neither can you, if you search out the truth.

Cricket. Nea, you neede not, wee knowe it, wee know it.

Phile. Peace boye.

Crick. I am kild with this word boye.

Muso. Sirra search you them Crickett.

Crick. Nea, if I search not every hole hange me, and saye I am an Onion. Come sirra you porter letts see your sacke, open it you knave.

1 *Porter.* Knave, how many such knaves doe your ffather keepe?

Crick. Open it or &c.

2 *Porter.* Open it, I will open it.

1 *Port.* I sir, you shall have it opened.

Crick. what shall I give a bushell for theise coles?

3 *Port.* They be sold already.

Crick. whats here? your markett is spoyled, Coles turned into Corne.

Phile. A strange metamorphosis. |

p. 33 *Muso.* So strange that it will turne him into the Jayle.

Cole. By what authoritie?

Phile. By a writt from Mr Rector.

Crick. I, come Mr Coleby, you must be my prisoner.

Cole. Nea, good Gentlemen.

Phile. How now, who hath the witt now? alas we are simple fellowes, wee can doe nothing but that wee see done before, it is a marvell you did not teach us this? Come bringe them away, Ile teach you a tricke ere wee part with you, as shall cost you the setting on.

2 *Coll.* Nea, good Gentleman let mee goe, Ile doe any thing for you.

Crick. Come, come you Rogue followe us.

1 *Porter.* Nea, I beseech you, pardon us, we did but jest.

Muso. It is but a folly to intreate, we are inexorable, had I not heard it with my eares, I could scarcely have believed you could have invented [it], and shall I then pockett up theise cosonages for a fewe relentinge speeches? no, no, but what punishment the lawe will afford, be yee sure ye shall have it, carrie them away, I say.

2 *Port.* Good sweete fast Gentleman speake for us.

Crick. Downe, downe on your knees there good fellowes pray hartiely.

Phile. It is in vaine, I cannot neither will I pardon you.

Coleby. Alas, alas, that ever I was borne, what will become of my poore wife?

1244 fast MS. 'fact' altered to 'fast'

1 *Cole*. I care not. I hope my Master will beare my charges.

(*Exeunt omnes. Cricket & Musonius manent.*)

Crick. Nea Mr Musonius you must needes stay with mee, you shall not goe.

Muso. And I prethie good wagg, why must I beare the companie?

Crick. Nea, Ile have you intreate mee, I have it, I have it will pepper them.

Muso. Prethe good now impart it unto us.

Crick. well sir, first knowe, that I durst not stay you, but upon some extraordinarie occasions.

Muso. well sir, what ensues?

Crick. marrie sir, there is a good lustie arrant whore att this welsh Rogues house, and to be short, Mr Nifle meanes to coole his lust, and to doe some thing, within this houre he will come, I heard Tavy say, her was ferrie cood wench, cod be praysed and plessed for it.

Muso. Away you Rascall, it is impossible.

Crick. I cannot tell, but I am sure as I was watching for Mr Coleby, I heard a right downe match betwene Nifle and Tavy, this is it a man shall gett for doeing his endevour.

p. 34 *Muso*. Nea. I | prethe good man be not so Cholerike, I believe thee well, Ile watch this night. O that I had but a writt now. I goe presently and raise Mr Rector, and fetch one, thou good lad shalt be lingering hereabout to stea Philenius and his company if they come, doe good Crickett I pray thee.

Crick. ô god Mr Musonius make hast, I play my part, ô Musonius, god send thee good fortune to send the Lord Governour of the gaile into the jayle. (*Exit Musonius.*) mee thinks I see the villaine how pittifully he looks when he is taken in his lechery. but how shall I passe away this night? it is very cold, ffaith Ile goe and gett mee a heate, lett mee see, what is the watchword? knocke thrice, call Tavy, and I burne. Tavy, Tavy.

Tavy. Howe is here keepe such a rip rap at her doore?

Crick. I burne, open the dore.

Tavy. nea, her arship shall quench her pye and pye, her will putt her fire out, come in, come in.

Crick. I, I, Ile sett you in with a powder.

(*hee fells him.*)

Tavy. Scald peggerly knave lett her purne, and her serve her such an other pranke, her will never serve cod more, well her will in and shutt her tore, her shall not purne here. (*Exit.*)

Crick. God graunt, that my knavery keepe not Nifle out of dores, I would not for a world of treasures it should fall out so, but I knowe the lecherous knave will rangle hard before he will be denied, here he comes, Ile away and hasten the company. (*Exit.*)

1282 Musonius MS. 'Musonias'

ACTUS 3us. SCENA 5^{a}.

Niphle solus.

Nifle. mee thinks men in authoritie should not be moved with love as I am. I cannot tell the reason, but my wife pleaseth me not, I must naturallye goe abroad, of my Conscience, I thinke all magistrats are of my mynde, or else I am sure my mynde would not be so moved with it. but now what doe I meane to indanger my selfe? what if the gentle Athenians should knowe of it? were it not much to loose my good name? Stay Nifle stay, temper thy selfe Nifle, p. 35 temper thy selfe, | with chastitie, ô Nifle cannot, Niphle must needes to this geare, I and Nifle shall. why but Niphle thou must provide for the worst, I thou shalt, thou shalt, thou didst performe thy office and then they that dare lett them but touch Nifle, if they doe upon their owne perill be it. But why doe I stay from my delight? this [is] Tavies house, Ile knocke, here is all very closse, I must knocke thrice, Tavy, Tavy.

Tavy. who knockes att her dore?

Niphle. I burne, I burne.

Tavy. Lett her purne ant poxe and plague, and all te tevills in hell on her, ant her will, her shall fetch no fire here, water here.

Nifle. what a knave is this? I tell thee knave, tis I the head of this Cittie.

1321 touch MS. 'tough'
1330 fire here Should these words be omitted?

Tavy. why shittie knave, her will knocke her on the head, coson her so againe, and say Tavy was a ferie foole, lett her pip pap where her list for Tavie.

Niphle. what a knave is this to speake so lowd? why Tafy it is Nifle.

Tavy. I, tell her a tale of a tubb, so her was even now, was her not trow? yet get her packing or her will sett her packing with a poxe.

Niphell. This it is to trust welsh vagabonds, lust pricks on sore, I must intreat. nea Tavy, what meanest thou to use mee so? I am thy friend Nifle.

Tavy. I her goot friend, preck her pate, ferie cot friend, her vill gett her downe, her vill take her velch sword, her vill have her ploode.

Nifle. what a Rogue is this? preethe doe but looke out and see.

Tavy. See, I and so putt out her eyes, her vill take her sweard, putt on her puff shirken, on her skull, not take her heeles, her vill have her plud.

Nifle. why what ayles thou to be so scrupulous? come prethee letts come in.

Tavy. Hoe is here? ho keepe her out; lett her looke upon her.

Nifle. why Tavy what meanest thou to use mee thus?

Tavy. Marrie come in ant follow her, ant her can tell her, her was abust before, but come ant her will make her quiett.

Nifle. Is shee there?

Tavy. I, I, follow her, her shall finde her.

Nifle. This is somewhat, yett make all sure I prethe. (*Exeunt.*)

ACTUS 3us. SCENA 6^a^.

Musonius. Cricket, with others. Purcus. Trot. Spooner. Searchers.

Cricket. See now how I am for theise hoyden Athenians iffaith, now I have the same Scottish dagger,
p. 36 I nimbd | it the fineliest you would not thinke, I cutt it from my Tutors side as he was leaning on his window lookinge on a booke, and he never perceived mee. Now have at you, you slaves you, heigh brave lads heigh.

Muso. I had no sooner gott to Mr Rectors lodging, but presently he gave it mee in his bed, and greatly commended our studies. lett us see what company wee have here; what shall wee doe with this little Ape amonge us?

Crickett. ffoh Mr Musonius ther's a question! why Ile doe more att the hoisting of a Clowne, then the greatest looby of them all.

Muson. I but you must trudg homeward. why they will say wee are all boyes, if they should see you, come you must be gone.

Crick. I must be gone, and here is a great stocke, that hath no more mettall in him then your whelpe, and hee must goe, because he is a litle bigger then I, and I must be gone.

1366 *Purcus* MS. 'Parcus' Cp. 1600, 1602, 1606, etc.
1383 *Muson.* MS. 'Moson.'

Muso. How this boy prates. you will play the Rakehell.

Crick. Nea, if you thinke not well of my company, I will not trouble you. this is all that I have for helping to this oportunitie, Ile make a shewe, but I will not leave you so. (*Hee goes by a little.*)

Muso. Are you gone? fare you well. I wonder why Philenius stayes so longe.

ACTUS 3us. SCENA 7^{a}.

Philenius and his company.

Phile. ffaith, Mr Coleby hath but cold lodging, but mee thinks, I see some Companie before us, my Masters you must stand to it, here is some false knaves abrode. Hoe is there?

Muso. A friend.

Phile. The word. downe with him.

Muso. Nay Philenius, hold, hold, it is Musonius.

Phile. Musonius, if thou hadst not spake, wee had made you tast of Clublawe, but why are you here? I wonder thou didst not followe us.

Muso. Thou maist presume some urgent occasion hath detayned mee.

Phile. I prethee lett us knowe.

Muso. To make any discourse would be too tedious, only marke the event and follow mee. I tell the I am the Officer, this is the house, who is within here, open the dore.

1399 *Philenius* MS. 'Phileius'

Tavy. what will her peate downe her toore? who is here?

Muso. Marry wee come from Mr Rectors with authoritie to search your house for certeine suspitious persons.

Tavy. Ho, Mr Nifle, oh the search, the Rectors search is come, what will you doe?

Nifle. Search? Alas what shall I doe? keepe them out.

Tavy. Catts plood can her tell how? away.

p. 37 *Phile.* what | shall wee attende all this night upon this Rogues pleasure? burst ope the dore.

Tavie. Nea, her shall not need, be not over hasty, what will her needs search, py codd her skorne to keepe pip pap in her house.

Muso. Come letts in.

Tavie. nay Shentlemen let her crave lett not above 2. or 3. in.

Muso. Prethee keepe the dore, lett none come in.

Tavie. Marry her doe so had need, her was loose a Coverlett and napkins.

Muso. Come letts see what strangers you have here, open that doore. how now, what wench is this?

Tavie. Is her sister.

Phile. nay if shee be his sister lett us in to. (*They enter in.*)

Tavie. what a poxe will her lett all the towne in?

Muso. Rise huswife, and make your selfe readie.

Luce. ffor your pleasure sir?

Muso. This is strange he should escape us.

Phile. Nea, we must finde him out.

Nifle. Ô god how am I persecuted by a company of gentle Athenians! ô would to god I had kept my selfe with the good man. I had never byn so troubled. ô lust, lust, what danger am I come into by thy procuring, but what shall I doe, whither shall I goe, that I may hide my selfe? ô that men in authoritie should be in such adversitie, lett mee see, heeres a tubb. Ile creepe in here, they will never suspect it.

ffinis Act. 3. *Scenæ* $7^{\text{mæ}}$.

ACTUS 3us. Scena 8va.

Cricket.

Cricket. whats there creeping into a tubb? I hold my life Mr Burgomaster hath scapt the search, I am glad I came backe againe, Ile stande by and say nothing.

A wench in the tubb. Nea good gaffer, doe not hurt mee, I am a poore beggar wench, for the passion of god doe not beate mee, I did not knowe it was your tubb.

Nifle. Hold thy peace good wench, I doe not meane to hurt thee.

Wench. Ôh you will, you will, good God what shall become of mee?

1454 adversitie MS. 'distresse' (underlined) and 'adversitie' written in the same hand in the margin.

1456 $7^{\text{mæ}}$ MS. '7^{mi}' 1461 and say MS. 'and say and say'

Nifle. I tell thee I will not, lye still, and I will give thee two pence, for Gods sake lye still.

Muso. You had as good certifie us where hee is, youle injurie your selfe more then you thinke of.

Tavy. As cod shall helpe her soule, her vas runne away.

Phile. Come letts after him, wee may overtake him ere hee come att his house.

Muso. Content. Why you litle villaine, what make you here?

Cric. ffaith I could not loose your company, for I came backe againe presently, but where is hee? where is hee?

Muso. you [are] a fine boy, I durst venture my p. 38 life hee was | never here.

Crick. Come, come, he'res a jeast, my credite was never cract yet, and must it now be called into question? It stands upon my good name fame and reputacion. I cannot indure it, well will you lett mee be the Capteine of the search?

Phile. Away, away, dost deride us?

Cric. Nea, by this good candle light, I meane plaine honestie. turne it unto mee and Ile find him out Ile warrant you.

Muso. Nea, then good boy to it, letts see thy skill.

Crick. Hold Chopper, there Lockwood, a plage on that Curre, hee lyes out villonestly, breake his legges: here, here, here, Daynty the dogg trayled him out, there hee goes, a start, a start, helpe, helpe.

Phile. How now, whats here ?

Crick. Heres the game, but it will not rise.

Muso. weele offer it faire playe, out with it.

Nifle. Hold your hands for Gods sake, two wofull wretches nere starved for cold.

Crick. The game is turned into 2. Ôh Mr Burgomaster, God give you joy of your bedfellowe.

Phile. Nea good sir, goe not away, w'ele beare you company, now I assure you, I am very sorrie twas our fortunes to trouble you, neverthelesse Ile make you amends, ere I part with you.

Crick. nea, I'le keepe thee.

Wench. nea, good Gentlemen, lett mee goe, I had beene gone long a goe, if it had not byn for him, hee kept mee in so hee did.

Crick. what did hee to thee ?

Phile. nea, if hee like so well of your companie, I will not offer him that injurie to part you so soone, you shall goe togither, wee will leave you as wee founde you.

Crick. In a tub, heres a tale of a tubb indeede.

Nifle. why, I hope you found mee doeinge no ill, but executing my Office. Are wee not straightly charged to looke to vagabonds and beggars ? and shall I then be taunted and mocked, for creeping into a tubb to pull out a beggar wench, that hath offended the lawe ?

Wench. Truely gaffer, hee meant no such thinge, hee bad mee ly still, and hee would give mee two pence.

Crick. what a two peny queane?

Muso. How say you Mr Burgomaster, is this the executing of your office? is this the cause you walke the streets so late att night?

Nifle. well goe to, mocke on, and see what will come of it, it is not the wordes of a raskallie wench can justifie that which you have done, Ile make you repent, that ever you did injurie mee in this sort.

p. 39 *Phile.* It may be so, if you could finde the meanes how. but not withstanding whatsoever | happen unto us wee be not dismayed, nea looke upp, looke upp, wee have cause to sorrow not you. Now on my credit, it was a deede of great pollicie, better in a tubb man, then in a Churchyard as some of you have done.

Muso. yet best of all in the Jayle. will it please you to see your chamber sir? it is readie.

Nifle. what I to the Jaile? Am not I Mr Nicholas Nifle that can commaund both Jaile and Jayler? And shall I then be led as prisoner to the Jayle. ô that I had but my men att my heeles, I would trye who should goe to the Jayle.

Crick. you to the Jayle, as though men in your place have not byn in the Jayle, for some suchlike knavery.

Phile. Nea, good Mr Nifle, doe not refuse our kindnes, what wee doe is for your good; Ile' assure you the prisoners cannot chuse but thinke well of you. what is a groat for a garnish? Upon my life, if you thinke much att it your sweete heart will paye halfe of it.

1535 what MS. 'what what'   1559 your MS. 'you'

Muso. Come, come, you shall goe.

Wench. And shall I too?

Crick. I marrie Master Burgomaster and you shall have both one chamber.

Phile. I marrie shall you. this tis to trust to a welsh Raskall, that for any light gaine will sell his owne father, is it possible hee should reveale your secretts?

Nifle. Is it even so? If I be not even with him, lett Nifle be no more himselfe. Never trust mee, I scorne you and all such villaines, I will not goe, I will answere you by the lawe.

Muso. Nea, you shall answere it. youle goe?

Nifle. No.

Muso. will you be carried then sir? I, I, because hee is a man of state it shall be so, take him my masters and putt him into his tubb of state and bravely on your shoulders carrye him with triumph thorough the streets.

Nifle. Help Cittisens, help, helpe. (*hee is put in the tubbe.*)

Crick. would you have more help sir? I warrant you theis will carry you well enough.

Phile. lett him have his mistris with him for company. (*the wench is [put] in the tubb.*)

Crick. Come Masters, come you great asse to hoist her up.

Wench. Lord, shall I be kild? shall I be kild?

Nifle. Shall shee be carried with mee to disgrace mee too?

p. 40 *Muso.* To disgrace you no, but least | you should be proud of this great Triumph, after the ancient manner, you shall have this poore servant to be carried with you, that you may be humbled att the sight of her, well now you may marche awaye.

Crick. ô most stately, most fine, gallant, witty Burgomaster, brave Diogenes in a tubb, this is the dayntiest sport, this doth mee good at the verye harte.

Muso. my masters, goe to Tavies house and bringe the queane after us, Ile goe see Mr Burgomaster fast layd upp, Purcus looke to it, shee shall be your charge.

(*Exeunt.*)

Purcus. wele' bring her sir. what ho youle come there?

ACTUS 3us. SCENA 9^{a}.

Enter Searchers, Tavie, Luce.

Tavie. I pray let her stay a litle, the candle is out.

Purc. Come away I say.

Luce. youle give me leave I hope, to make mee readie; brother I did not thinke I should have byn disquieted in your house thus.

Bromly. How the pox came you to be of kindred? shee speakes not in the throat as you doe.

Tavie. Her was petter prought up, thanke her cood uncle Morgan.

Pur. what must wee stay all night?

Tavie. I pray her arships be not angrie, her vas come py and py.

1616 not Inserted over the line in the MS.

Purc. Bring her out as shee is.

Tavie. Come sister Luce, her make the Shentlemen angree, vill doe her no harme I warrant her.

Luce. Lett the proudest of them all doe mee any harme if they dare, I pray you bid your companie come out, there are some of them have filched my gloves there and my buske point, I hope you will see mee have them againe.

Tavie. yes vas warrant her selfe.

Luce. I doe but jeast, I want nothing but a litle sleepe, faith Gentlemen you doe mee ronge, you awaked mee out of the finest dreame I had this twelve moneths.

Bromly. ffaith Luce, what was thy dreame? |

Luce. ffaith lad, that my Ringe was drawne on thy p. 41 finger, but thou shalt never have my maidenhead.

Brom. I thinke so indeed.

Trott. I faith, I warrant thee, shee is one of those huswives.

Luce. True Roger, your shinns burne.

Spon. Luce, Luce, thou knowest Bridget Boulton.

Luce. Jesus, sweete heart art thou there? I did not see the before. I hope thou wilt not carrie mee to prison. (*Shee kisses him.*)

Trot. Sponer, art thou not ashamed? Truely I would not for 100^{li} shee should knowe mee so.

Luce. Knowe thee? Didst not come to mee once, when thou hadst a single groat in thy purse, and I would not, and thou offeredst to pawne mee thy hatt-bond?

Trott. ffie on thee, fie on thee, but thy tongue is no slander.

Spon. Bromly, kill her with a jeast, putt her downe in her owne kind.

Brom. Ile have a flinge at her.

Luce. A flinge at mee gods body, I see your hart out first.

Brom. My meaning is not so.

Luce. Is it so bobie? Then keepe your winde to coole your pottage; but what would it saye, if it could speake now? lett us heare it ruffle in Rhetorke.

Brom. I saye, I account it none of my meanest misfortunes to have mett with the in regard—

Luce. ffaith, this fellow hath studied playes. well, well, didst ever see Orlando furioso sirra?

Brom. No, but I have seene Layis now I see thee.

Luce. what is shee?

Brom. a whore.

Luce. Gods nayles a whore, take that Raskall (*shee strickes him*).

Pur. nea if you cannot hold your hands, come alonge.

Luce. I come alonge, you are all Raskalls.

Tavy. Pray Shentlemen, hurt her not, come, come, her cannot keepe her tongue, cannot kive good wordes to them?

Purc. Nay, lett her alone, wee will Charme her tongue well enough, Drab as shee is.

Tavy. ant please her arship, no drab her hope.

1658 Rhetorke Query 'Rhetorike'

Luce. Goe seeke you drabs with a vengance, you knowe them well enough.

Tavy. Peace; what hast tou to doe to metle with other folkes houses?

Luce. I care for none of them all, and if they doe they may goe to the next house and may have a noble wench, a Royall one in a silke gowne, come downe in a wagon, they can lett her see, I warrant you.

Brom. Come, come, away then, and shee shall followe. because you saye I have studied playes, I apoint you torch bearer to the Devill.

Sponer. | Luce, shall I speake for thee? p. 42

Luce. I thanke god I neede none of you to speake for mee, its knowne well enough what I am, but that there is none of my friends here, I should not be used thus; if Mr Musonius were here himselfe, I knowe hee is a kinde Gentleman. (*Shee weepes.*)

Brom. Sirra, observe a good humor, even now jeastinge, then scolding, now crying, you shall see her change, 20. to one, you shall see her sicke or with childe.

Trot. Ôh is your stomacke come downe?

Tavy. Alas her was ever a ferie kinde honest wench, doe na cry so Luce, her was not use to rise so soone.

Luce. ffaith, I am but a foole to crye, it is nothing but my kinde hart that doth mee harme, but ant please god Ile' never doe as I have done.

Spoon. what wilt thou then leave being in so good doeinges?

1699 was ever MS. 'was ever was ever'

Luce. Thou art a wagg efaith, I cannot chuse but laugh att you.

Brom. Now exit laughing, what rules next?

Purc. Come, now you have had sport enough, alonge with us.

Luce. I faith, I could make better sport in bed, I praye thee lett mee goe.

Purc. Then wee shall never have done, come away come.

Luce. Nea, I pray the sweete hart, faith I am sicke, I had such a suddaine qualme come over my stomacke, ô, I praye thee good brother give mee some Aquavitæ.

Brom. I told you, shee would be sicke.

Purc. you shall not neede Aquavitæ, you shall be quickned with a whipp.

Luce. with a ffoxe taile, will you not? but you may save that labour, my husband hath done it before. I am quicke already efaith.

Spoon. what hast thou gott a husband now?

Luce. I have one, if he were here, hee would not turne his head from the prowdest of you all.

Spoon. why where is hee?

Luce. It is well knowne where hee is. Mr Tooky knowes he went the voyage with Captaine Carifeild, but the worst lucke myne, I have not seene him this 3. yeares daye.

Brom. How camst thou to be with child by him then?

Luce. well enough, he came in one night when the shipp stayed for him, and was gone ere morning.

I never sawe him, god is my Judge, you shall not take mee in a lye, I warrant you.

Brom. what a brasen fac't whore is this, ô damnd lye.

Luce. Dost call mee whore that have | a husband? p. 43
I tell thee, I am as honest as thy mother (thou bastard thou) or any of thy kindred, goe thy waye.

Tavie. nay cods plude be to playne nowe. cannot keepe her tongue a litle? I hope her arships will peare with a foolish wench, speake in her anger her cannot tell what.

Spon. Lett us please her againe.

Trott. Content.

Spon. Luce.

Luce. what sayst thou love?

Spon. Thou couldst be content not to goe.

Luce. I faith I care not whether I went or no, so my brothers 2. barrells of stronge beere were drawne I have under my hand.

Brom. why thou [hast] drawne 2. barrells to night for him, hast thou not?

Luce. Hoe told you so?

Brom. Mr Nifle.

Luce. Kisse Mr Nifle behind, I defie thee and all thy company, saye your worst you can by mee.

Trott. wee may as well forbare truely, for wee shall never make thee better.

Luce. why what is shee milkesop what is shee?

1744 peare MS. 'peace'
1753 brothers MS. 'bothers'

Brom. why thou art a Camero, a punck, in plaine termes a mercenarie whore.

Luce. Thou saist like an arrant arrant Rogue. didst thou ever knicke knocke with mee?

Tavy. ffor the love of cod Luce hold thy tongue, her cannot tell what her doe tincke.

Luce. who should make mee hold my [tongue] they?

Purc. not wee, but the Clericals shall, come Helpe masters.

Luce. ôh my sides, gods death, if my child miscarry, Ile make the proudest of you looke through a hemping windowe.

ACTUS 3us. SCÆNA 10^{a}.

Enter Musonius. Philenius.

Muso. what a noise is here? whats the matter with her? why stand you longe with her?

Luce. ô Mr Musonius, they will kill, they will kill mee.

Muso. Nea, I warrant thee, thou plaiest thy prises now, carry her awaye I saye.

Luce. you Gentlemen, you dogges, you tatterd ragtailes, you are all knaves, rogues, basterdly raskalls, and all the fathers, granfathers, great grandfathers, great great grandfathers, mothers, sisters, brothers, cosens, unckles, aunts were all hanged, and so will you

1778 *Musonius* MS. 'Mosonius'

be, like dambd villaines as you are, and besides—*Exit.*

Muso. Come you awaye to, Sirra.

Tavy. Ant please her arship, there is none to keepe her house.

Muso. well sirra w'ele talke with you | to morrow, p. 44
then you shall knowe your punishment.

Tavye. Thanke your arship.

Muso. This night is almost spent, wee will take 2. houres sleepe upon our bedds, then wee will goe to Mr Rector to knowe his pleasure, for the dismounting of those repining drudges.

Phile. Il'e to him as soone as he is up, I dare presume he will doe it, he is inclined to it already, but now letts awaye. (*Exeunt.*)

ACTUS 4us. Scæna 1^{a}.

Enter Rumford. Catch.

Rumf. By the messe, I have byn with my good billie Colbie, hee sweares hee will not putt it up, and told mee, believe mee, hee would goe out prison. So faith, wee have laid our poles in Colbies storehouse and believe [mee,] wees thwake their Jackes. See here is Catch, marrie hee's a good strammell lad, Il'e lett him know all. hearst Tom. Catch? whither gangst Tom. now?

Catch. I must goe fetch a cleane shirt for Mr Burgomaster in prison.

Rumf. Nea, faith wees send some other, thous staye with mee.

Catch. why I praye you?

Rumf. Because I take thee to be a bonny lad and a good honest fellowe, as any of our towne, and because I thinke th'oule tell no living creature, Ile tell thee.

Catch. ffaith, for my honesty, I am as honest as any man of my office can bee, I thinke I am no blab of my tongue, but sir, whats the matter?

Rumf. Thou canst tell how theis Jackes, gentle Athenians misused us and imprisoned Mr Burgomaster and Mr Colbie, the scrubbes are so perke now, if wee doe not take them downe a hole lower, the slaves will crowe over us.

Catch. Take heed what you doe, they are seene in the blacke art, they will make us all daunce naked.

Rumf. The dele they will, and thou'le take my counsaile, wees goe thacke them, wees make their coats yelpe.

Catch. So wee may pull downe houses on our heades, and be well lamb'd our selves, but I am but one, and Ile helpe you in any thinge.

Rumf. thou sayes well, thou hast true bloud in thee, thou knawest to night is holy daye, and there will be waster play, and theres not a gentle Athenian but will gange thether, and when they are there, wees so clapper clawe them, that wees make their sides warke.

Catch. But they have pestilent things called Clubbes.

Rumf. Poe, poe, wee have the same too, and mickle

longe staves, and all the ladds in the towne shall be mustered, and faith wees pay them | backe and side. p. 45

Catch. well sir wee must not spare, but lett the towne knowe of it

Rumf. ffaith, Ile gange and tell our ladds of it, and thous gett thy companions and tell them of it, harke thou mee.

Catch. well you were best to be gone quickly and make hast, but where are your weapons ?

Rumf. why here in Colebies store house, gang thou that way, and Ile gang this and meete here againe.

Catch. Ile goe first to my fellowe Tavie, and tell him of it, and then Ile provide all the youthes on this side of the towne, and bring them to his house.

Rumf. I doe, doe my bonny lad.

ACTUS 4[us]. SCENA 2[a].

Enter Musonius. Mistrisse Colbie.

Mris Colbie. The filthy Runt can scarce reach upp to one of their heads with his staffe, and yett he must [be] Captaine of this enterprise, yet I am sory for nothing but that my husband (as Romford sayes) must come out of prison soone. and now forsooth wee have the staves laid up in his storehouse to beate the Gentlemen. I faith, I love them too well to suffer them to take any harme, and ifaith, Ile prevent them of their purpose, if I can but meete with Mr Musonius. and yonder he is, Ile harken what he sayes.

Muso. As soone as I awaked I sent Philenius to

Mr Rector for to informe him of our successe, and withall to procure the mechanicks might [be] dismounted and oftentymes our worthy Rector mencioned it unto mee, but thy fortunes Philenius answere my thoughts, and wee shall oppose to our gratious aspect the Image of true humilitie. but now as I suppose this is the daye wee should be clubd, I am come to heare the certeinty of my gossip Colbye, twenty to one, shee will tell all in a passion. but yonder shee is, god save you Mistresse Coleby.

Mris Col. Mr Musonius, you come as just as Jermyns lippe, ô if yee had not come I had sent for you, come letts have a loving kisse.

Muso. must you needes have one? Ile never deny such a reasonable request.

Mris Col. Good lord reasonable, iffaith you are to reasonable, but why did yee [not] come the last night? effaith you are to blame, but I am as good as my word, I have learned out all their knaveries.

p. 46 *Muso.* and what | must wee be cudgeld?

Mris Col. I needes, for they are all preparing staves, and all are gone to gett the yonge youths of the towne to helpe, I warrant you they beginne the sport anone, if I were a man, I would take your part, never credit mee if I would not.

Muso. If thou wert a woman thou shouldest have more modestie, but sweete hart thou shouldest not. but I pray you, where doe they laye their staves?

1890 but why MS. 'by why'

1900 shouldest Query 'art' (the corruption being due to 'shouldest' above).

Mris Col. Rumford by my husbands apointment hath laid them up in my husbands store house.

Muso. Couldest thou but helpe us to them thou shouldest gaine unto thy selfe an æternall lover.

Mris Col. Should I indeed? ffaith it shall goe hard but I will.

Muso. If thou doest thou gaynest mee for ever.

Mris Col. well, Il'e doe it, never trust mee, if I doe it not, Ile see one of theis dayes what you will doe, but now I goe to my witts to performe my promise. within this houre come or send for them, all of our men will be a drinking, and so you may gett them away.

Muso. I pray you remember. *Exit* [*Mris C.*].

Muso. I, I this kindnes ever, who could want such an iniquitie for an instrument att such a tyme? att [such] an enterprise? inconstant flurts, that seeke to injurie their husbands beds in disclosing of secretts. but this is straunge Philenius meets mee not. I hope the Rector will not deny his suite, tending to the reformation of such Crymes as doth both prejudice both him and us. had it byn effected sooner, ere this they had byn made stoope, and with bending knees to shewe their submission.

Phi. Mr Rector hath dismist Colbie upon small consideracion, like enough that he might feele the greater smart, that he might procure, but Nifle is fast for a while; how now Musonius, what growne malecontent?

Muso. Ruminating of the successe.

1919 straunge MS. 'staunge' 1921 doth both Query omit 'both'
1927 procure Something is omitted perhaps.

Phile. Bury theis thoughts. our wills shall be accomplished, our Rector with unexpected willingnes effected speedily what I desired. hee gave mee his counsell and therewithall provided, that by his bills dispersed in every place intelligence might be had of his decrees. to testifie what I avouch to bee true, see heres one of them. read it I pray you.

(*hee gives him the bill.*)

Muso. To the Governors and Rulers of severall | p. 47 societies

[pp. 47 and 48 wanting (one leaf torn out).]

feare. p. 49

Tavie. Puff, foule knave, and you saucie Jacke doe not her knowe hoe her is, Catch ?

Catch. why are you not my fellow Serjeant ?

Tavie. Tell not vat her vas, but vat her es, her be now gallant Capten Tavie to knocke downe the shentle Athenians, make her give creat knocke rippe rappe rippe rappe, heigh Saint Tavie is a welsh man borne.

Catch. I hope youle lett mee be your Lefetenant.

Tavie. Lieutenant ? pegerly knave ! vas keepe her old office, pull of her cap, make rome with her masse, her will make her knowe herselfe.

Catch. Naye I hope you will not use mee so hardly.

Tavie. And her be humble, shalbe nere the worse.

Breck. Sure except there be great neede I will not strike one blowe, but if wee could but recover our sale againe, wee were happy men, for wee are halfe undone by this discomininge.

Spruce. But that I am a man of peace, ôh how I could Captaine it. But I thinke Tavie hath byn in the warres, he may serve it sufficienly.

Breck. ffaith Tavie you are brave.

Tavie. what a poxe call her Tavie, her is petter man then her. doe her know not Captaine ? Rumford made her leader.

Spruce. well see you performe your office.

Tavie. Pough, leave her prittle prattle. Captaine

1960 man of peace MS. 'man in peace'
1968 prittle MS. 'puttle'

Tavie knowe militarie discipline and service. ranke Puffe scald knave ranke, for cods, her will breake her pate else.

Rumf. Gods blessing of thy saule bonny ladd, faith I be thy Corporall.

Tavie. Nea, her shall be her Lieutenant, come Mr Brecknock and Mr Spruce must ranke and obey her Captaine. Catch shitten knave, goe in her place. Puffe here there was for you sawcie Jacke.

Puff. You are very lustie, youl doe little enough anone.

Tavie. Leave her pratling, come followe her, hight St Tavie St Tavie. follow her alonge, first lett her call Mr Colby. is Mr Coleby within ?

Colbie. yea marie is hee.

Tavie. what are the staves readie ?

Coleby. All in a readynesse.

Rumford. By my troth, Ise very glad you are
p. 50 come out of prison, I thought | you had byn in still.

Colbie. I thanke god, I gatt out presently, but it cost my purse soundly; and I live, Ile be even with them.

Rumf. I marry doe, if you be wise.

Tavie. Vell her all goe now to her house, and staye their a while in readinesse till the Athenians come abroad?

Rumf. I, I lett us gange crush a pott or two of Ale att thy house, there is as good as ever was turne over the tongue.

1996 turne Query 'turned'

Cole. Doe, Ile have a game att Tables with you in the meanetime.

Tavie. Come, and her shall drinke a Cuppe of good Methiglen and her please toe.

ACTUS 4us. SCENA 5^{a}.

Enter Musonius and his Company.

Muso. Sirs, I praye you be in a readines.

All. I warrant you.

Phile. The case stands even so, make your selves readie to take our parts against so base raskalls.

(*Mounsier the ffrenchman speakes.*)

Muso. wee knowe great affeccion towards us, else wee would not move you, in a matter of such importance.

Crickett. Have him? what should wee doe with him? heele runne awaye presently.

Mounsier. Dost thou saye so litle wagpastie? Cod me tanke you alwaye for your curtesie, your name is written in my hart, mee will so strike de scurvie rogues in de face, when mee was in ffrance me kill 2. or 3. men tere abuse mee, mee will cutt their throats.

Crickett. Durst thou so? that was well done.

Mouns. I pie my traunt, mee will trawe my tagger for your sake, mee love you verie well, scurvie rogue to sell Aquavitæ, shoes, breeches and dublett, and base knaves. shentle Athenians love vench, and take Tobaccoe ferie well. scurvie Rogues, Clownes.

2014 *Mounsier* MS. 'Mousier' 2023 take MS. 'take take'

Muso. Nea, Mounsier you shall see verye good knocking.

Crick. Iff hele come among the knocks, Ile be knocked for him.

Mounsier. Its [no] madder for datt, is a Child, be Cot, I tinke, no better cuffer in de world, de gentle Athenians stricke ferrie creat plow, is good fassion, mee tell you see a scholler de Paris beate verie prave Shentleman, so silke and velvett.

Phile. They be true harted fellowes.

Mouns. In truth, its fewe good fellowes, but tell so ven dis bee.

Muso. Presentlie.

Mouns. Twickly, twicklie, twicklie.

p. 51 *Crick.* well ffrenchman, you | make hast, but tell mee true, will not you be the first will runne awaye?

Mouns. Tell, vill not tine Tutor brich tine heash?

Muso. what Mris Coleby are you within?

Mris Coleby. I, I am as good as my word every whitt, make hast, praye have them awaye quicklie, for our men will come from tiplinge by and by. Ile goe in and give you them out.

Muson. Come, come, come, make hast.

Mris Colbye. Here, here, here, make hast (*they take them and carry them crosse over the stage*).

Mouns. Harke, what vench is dis? not drunke?

Crick. No, no, shee is one that loves a proper Gentleman. but nowe Musonius I would the sport would begin.

2031 is Query 'in' 2033 so Query 'in'
2037 Presentlie MS. 'Prensentlie' 2041 heash Clearly corrupt.

Muso. They will not staye longe, but hearest thou lad? thou must use thy witt and take occasion to beginne the fraye.

Cricke. Lett mee alone, Ile prove an excellent swaggerer.

Phile. why, but Musonius this will be counted a kinde of cosening policie.

Muso. Noe, thou art deceived, for either it will shewe their sottishnes, and in us it will be deemed folly not to accept such an occasion, whereby wee may with ease overcome them, neither is the matter of so small importance: they surpassing us in number and thou mayst be sure they will [not] be altogither unprovided.

Phile. In the meane time while they come, wele stand by, as spectators of their sport.

ACTUS 4us. Scena 6a.

Enter Tavie, Rumford, Brecknock, Colbye with others.

Tavie. Now is tyme to goe, come lett her all stand here about till the shenerall behiett.

Colebie. Goe then, if all hold, Ile be even with them for imprisoning the bad utterance of my Coles.

2071 *Brecknock* MS. 'Brecknocky' *others* MS. 'other others'
2073 till the shenerall behiett MS. 'till the she ner all be hiett' See Note.

2075 imprisoning the bad utterance Query 'imprisoning [me for] the bad utterance'

Rumford. And I for my cause, that the strange theeves did hericke from mee in Lent.

Brek. I beseech god wee have good fortune, for I drempt of water last night.

Crick. Thou alwaies dreames.

Rumf. That's [as] if wee should over whelme, but thats the spite, our Master Nifle is fast.

p. 52 *Crick.* You | would wish that you were there too.

Cole. ffoe, foe, he must not be seene in this enterprise, but lett us be gone Mr Rumford. how this Tavie is changed! all this mirth is gone on a hily day night, and how whist the towne is!

Muso. Thou liest, it roareth with fooleries.

Rumf. why I have seene in my dayes sicke plaie, that all the gentle Athenians ha come and looked on our ladds.

Breck. I, I, there was some good fellowship then; but shall wee have noe sport? my Peter is a pretie boy, he will play with any boy of his bignes in the towne.

Crick. And thou the foole with any of thy bignes.

Muso. Lett us goe about them that they take occasion to rangle.

Rumf. Nea, my lad will twacke his side, Ile hold a pott of Ale, my ladd will give him the first thwacke.

Mouns. Sir de rogue drinke all.

Cole. Ile lay a pint of wine on Brecknocks lad.

Rumf. Ile take it, call him forth.

2077 hericke I can make nothing of this word.

2086 Tavie Query 'towne' hily day Query 'holy day'

Tavie. Lett her prepare her place.

Breck. Peter, Peter I saye, bring out the Cudgells there.

Crick. what will Peter doe?

Peter. Here they be Sir, no body will play Sir.

Muso. Yes more then thou expectest.

Rumf. Yes lad, your playfellowe Jockie.

Jockie. I Master, Ile twacke his side.

(*Spectators enter in.*)

Breck. Come shake hands first.

Rumf. I thats gamester like, rome, make rome Gentlemen.

Peter. Have att you.

Jockie. Nea, spare not.

Rumf. well done Jockie, that was a good thwacke.

Breck. Nea, he got nothing by that, to him againe Peter.

Colebie. Before god, you are the unruliest fellowes that ever I see, you must doe what you list.

Crick. This fellow is a pretie magistrate.

Cole. In faith, tho be prettie boyes.

Muso. Dost not see how artificially they begin to picke the quarrell?

Phile. I wonder the Gentlemen have deferd it so longe.

Breck. To him Peter my lad, ô my lad Peter had the best.

Rumf. well done bonny lads.

Breck. I come, come be friends, letts have some other.

Peter. Ile carrie the Cudgells, none will playe.

ffoots. Ile plaie about, which waye must I hold the Cudgells?

Crick. Doe you marke the concert?

Cole. Thou knowest well enough. (*They play.*)

p. 53 *Jockie.* what a great bobie is this to plaie | with such a litle lad!

Cole. what, will no bodie take up against him?

Adam. See, see what I can doe.

Coleby. Keepe out there, keepe out, those Athenians spoyle all you that are plaiers, make rome with Cudgells.

Cricket. It were best for you to take your shakles or Mr Burgomasters club.

Muso. Or your welsh breath.

Tavie. Make rome pie Cod her will sett her out with a pox.

Rumf. Make rome Gentlemen, you gamesters what bobies you be.

Adam. wee doe what wee can. (*one making rome strikes Cricket.*)

Cricket. You will logger head, dare you stricke mee?

ffotts. And if thou wert ten times better.

Muso. what will you offer us this violence?

Tavie. her will leave prating, will her not?

Phile. They shewe themselves to be barbarous.

Rumf. Nea, but thous best gett thee packinge.

Crick. Mr Musonius, can you abide theis opprobrious termes? lett mee Combatt that Northen tieke.

2147 club Query 'tub'

Romf. Heres thou mee Jacke, Ile make my litle boy whip thee for all thy title tatle, but you lads gett you gone.

Phile. Awaye base drudges, threaten us?

Muso. wee scorne your words and doe esteeme them as basely as your selves.

Rumf. wees garre you tast our Clubbes.

Tavie. Goots plude, scorne her upon her vilde pride.

Colebie. you shall not thinke to crowe over us as you have done.

Mounsier. In traunt is not good boxe.

Breck. you had as good a kept your lodginge.

Muso. Alas poore men I pittie you.

Phile. They have no cause of envie.

Tavie. Cots plude must her tongue walke? goe fetch her wepon.

Rumf. I, by the messe, wees garr them loape.

Cole. will you goe with us? wees fetch that will garr them stand further. (*Exeunt.*)

Muso. Now thou seest in what gallant humor theis base Companions are, how in their owne thoughts they triumph.

Phile. They litle knowe in what readines wee are to receive them. but Crickett, call out our company.

Cricket. youle give mee leave to fight too?

Muso. I my boye.

2171 *Tavie* MS. 'Davie'

2182 wees fetch etc. Colby is probably speaking Rumford's dialect in joke, as Cricket speaks Tavie's, ll. 599, 600.

Crick. Come, come my masters, Clubs for theis Clounes here, Clubs. (*Enter with a companie of clubs.*)

Muso. My masters, wee must stande to it and spare none of them.

Phile. Lett your handes walke as freely as your tongues.

Mouns. See is my Club stronge?

Crick. It is too stronge for thy usage.

p. 54 *Tavie.* Cotts plude was her not in a fyne | taking? not a Club left, plude knaves, her vill gett her some in her house.

Rumf. Nea, is no matter, lett noe scrubbes scape.

Colebie. Oh what an arrant drab is my wife, shee hath made awaye all our weapons.

Muso. Come sirs, on theis, that meane to be on us.

Cole. wele but defend our selves.

Phile. Nea, is your heart soe quickly cold?

Rumf. what lads are you so pert? wele have att you.

Muso. you shall not neede, downe with them.

Rumf. Bonny lads take that. (*they fight all.*)

Muso. upon them follow.

(*Exeunt omnes, save Mounsier, whom Rumford catches.*)

Rumf. Away ffrench Curre, Ile hange thee.

Mouns. I say nothing to you, lett mee alone, be quiett, is not so well jeast.

Rumf. Nea, Ile paye thee good faith. (*Exeunt.*)

Tavie. Lett her goe, lett her goe, her will foresweare armes.

Catch. To it Tavie.

2213 *Exeunt* MS. 'Exunt'

Tavie. Cots plud, looke to your selfe.

(*hee runnes awaye.*)

Rumf. wayes mee, Ise braind ô well a day.

(*Musonius striks downe Brecknock and Coleby and they crie* Wee are slayne, some pittie on us for gods sake.)

Phile. ffie, pitty, you have no need of pittie, beate them well, what corps here? see authoritie in so lowe estate.

Coleby. ô Lord Gentlemen, wee beseech you to pardon us, wee have offended.

Muso. Away you villains, pardon? doe you seek to rule over us?

Breck. Sweet lads forgive us, you shall never take us in the like offence.

Phile. Gett you gone you drudges, must you be swagerers?

Catch. Jesus, how my head akes.

Rumf. ôh, howe sore my braines are.

Puffe. Thanke you good Gentlemen, that you lett mee goe awaye alive, I am so bruised, that I cannot rise, if I might have a hundred pounds. But Ile creepe home as well as I can.

Crick. Be gone, you false Rogue. Ho Mr Musonius, did you ever see a man of better resolution then I am?

Musonius. you are a gallant indeed, but where is Mounsier?

2227 see Query 'did you ever see'

2231 pardon? do you seek to rule over us? (Or ône might read 'pardon do you seek? to rule over us?') MS. 'pardon, do you see to rule over us?'

Crick. why, sir, hee is lying under a stall, for gods stand by, here he comes.

Mouns. In varte, mee glad all de Clownes be beate, come Puffe, come Rogue.

Puff. Nea, good Mounsier.

Crick. See how the villaine dominers over the drybeaten slave, that can neither stirre hand nor foote.

Mouns. Come Rouge de Scurvie Clowne, call me ffrench dog, make loose dynner, laugh att mee speake, give no vine, sett mee among te scubbes.

Puff. Nea, good Mounsier, I was halfe slayne before, ô lord I bestowed the best I had on you.

Mouns. Thou liest rouge, scurvie rascall, abuse brave Cavelers, gentle Athenians, take Tobaccoe very p. 55 well, come | roug, para te ad supplicium.

Puff. Nea, good Mounsier hold your hands, I have wife and children.

Mouns. Lett mee rid tine wife, and make litle children: mee so scorne tine wife, is no good kisse, no good face, is blacke as Inke, abuse mee scurvie Puff, fatt rouge, impudent rouge.

Puff. Nea, for saint Dennis good ffrench man.

Mouns. Goe, goe, mee vill ripe tine horse, tit no matter for tut Marcus Tullio Ricero non facit lectio hodie, profecto ego volo te vapulabor.

Puff. This is to fall into a ffrenchmans hands, I prethee lett mee goe.

2271 ripe Query 'ride'

2271–2 tit no matter for tut Query 'tis no matter for tat' Cp. 643.

Mouns. Scurvy Clowne me stricke de in de face.

Muso. How now Mounsier, how have you sped?

Mounsier. By god brave, is gallant, mee have kild 2. 3. 4. 5. it myne Club looke.

Musonius. you have done couragiously. Mounsier, lett him goe, I preethee.

Mouns. ffor your sake, goe rouge, villaine.

Crick. ô monstrous! what a lye is that! as soone as ever the fraye began, hee gott and hidd himselfe in a Coblers stall, if a gentle Athenian came, he was a gentle Athenian, if any hoydon Athenian came, presently hee was hoyden Athenian, till all was done, and then hee mett Puff and came thus domineringe over him.

Mounsi. Goe you lye, dis not true, de little scurvy knave abuse mee.

Muso. you see hee is a Child you must pardon him.

Phile. But Musonius what blowes hast thou had in the scirmige?

Muso. ffaith none, but a Butcher lent mee a fillip over the shoulders with a Cleaver, but I mett him, I owe him nothinge.

Phile. ffore god, I am weary with beating of Brecknocke, the asse cried out and said hee was an old man, and cald mee sweete facet Gentleman, that I could not for pittie cudgell him.

Muso. I warrant thee, they will not be so ready to meete Club lawe, but I wonder they yield no more att their discommininge, I thought it would have dasht this enterprise.

Phile. why, would you have it worke in an instant? they quake already, thou shalt see how they will stoope, when tyme hath shewed how powerfull it is. But why stand wee here? lett us to our lodgings, and joye of the event.

Crickett. Ile doe nothing all this night, but singe songes and Catches.

Muso. So it is good.

ffinis Actus 4^{ti}. *Scenæ* $5^{tæ}$. |

p. 56 ACTUS 5us. SCENA 1^{a}.

Enter Puff solus.

Puff. well, my masters, is this the fruits of an office? Serjeant quoth you, I would I had byn a Surgeon, I had got more by this fray, then I shall gett by Arrests this 9. moneths. This is a company of haire-braynd fellowes, that cannot live quietly themselves, nor yet lett others. Before, I could have gone into lodgings, and fetcht as much beere as could have sufficed my whole house almost. Now, if I looke but in their lodgings, they presently crye out of mee, and are readye to laugh mee out of my clothes, and when I come home, my wife hath never a penny, and shee sware shee would not take any. ô horrible! what will become of us? the poore Coblers and Taylers are almost starved, and doe so crye out of the Burgesses of the [town]. well, Ile be so bold as to tell Mr Burgomaster of it. Now they shall be dismissed, my fellow

2323 fetcht MS. 'fetch'

Catch is gone before. But Tavie the welsh Rogue is turned Cogging for his knaverie, They say, hee betrayed Mr Burgomaster, but I am glad of it as if one had given mee 100^{li}, the rascall will gett more by Cogging then halfe a hundred of us. well, Ile followe Catch and I find not Mr Burgomaster more reasonable, Ile make suite to be an under Butler in some of their lodgings thats certeine, Ile end my dayes in a Cellar.

ACTUS 5us. SCENA 2^{a}.

Rumford solus.

Rumf. Gods death, what a dele? be mockt after this sort, and saye never a bitt to them: ha bonne whiniard Iffaith, if thou hadst beene by my side, and then the lurdains had so thwact mee as they did, Ise given them leave to take my head from my Cragg. Must sicke to steale all our poles away and then thwacke us when they had done, Nea, then the deale take mee, and they goe scotfree. effaith, Ile laye my legges on my bonny gray nagge and ride as longe as ere he is able to stand, Ile try all my good friends and spen all my goods to a gray groat, except I make them in a make taking. Ise gange my one selfe and kneele before the Duke, and Ise warrant you | Ise tell him a tale, I p. 57
make him heare; but the ganbelly Coleby told mee hee would gange with mee, Ise see, what hoe Coleby art thou within?

2348 then MS. 'they'

2354 make Query 'new' (the corruption being due to 'make' before or 'taking' following). The 'm' in the MS. is altered from 'n.'

2356 ganbelly Query 'gorbelly'

Coleby. I, I, what sayst thou ?

Rumf. make thee ready man, make thee ready, putt on thy best boots, and thy Cranckling spurrs. I pray thee make hast as fine as thou canst.

Coleby. I pray you come in and stay a lite, I am almost readie.

Rumf. mary and I will, make hast, make hast, gods sides man, what a dele is thy shone on and thou bound to ride ?

Cole. Tush, thou shalt not staye for mee.

Rumford. weele, weele, weele.

ACTUS 5us. SCENA 3^{a}.

Enter Nifle, Spruce, Catch, Puff.

They cry within. what shall wee be starved ? you undoe us all, I pray take some order.

Nifle. Keepe them backe there Serjeants, a poxe upon you all that I be thus bald upon still. I came but newly out of the Jaile, and now I am ready to be puld out of my clothes. Is it not a shame Mr Spruce, is it not a shame, that men in Authority should be cried out upon, by a company of vagabonds and slaves ? I see, I see, that in the end wee must yeild, if it be by theise meanes, confusion light upon them all, but heare you mee Mr Spruce, how shall wee persecute theis suits ? Shall wee complaine to the Duke of theis wronges ?

2381 light MS. 'ligh'

2382 persecute In the MS. 'persecute' is written with the contraction for 'per.' Perhaps a mistake for 'prosecute.' Cp. 2589.

Spruce. ffor myne owne part I knowe not, but it may be good and necessarie.

Nifle. I, I, if all were on my mynde, wee should spoyle their triumph, but doe you thinke it availeable ?

Spruce. Certaynly Sir, necessity makes it availeable, but I pray you Sir, take some other opinion.

Nifle. It is my meaning. Puff call forth Mr Brecknocke.

Puff. Ho Mr Brecknocke are you within ?

Breck. I, I, what would you ?

Puff. Mr Burgomasters worshipp would speake with your worship.

Breck. ô Sir, you be wellcome home.

Nifle. Nea Sir, I am come home, to find every thinge in such case tis in, but I praye you Sir, letts take our places to consult about theis affaires.

Breck. Nea Sir, I would I had byn with you, I had saved some of my bloud, which now I have lost.

Nifle. Thinke that the bloud is holy, that is spent in so good a cause. I my selfe | beeing as I am I have p. 58 ventred some thinge, and indeed no small crosses, but this may incourage us the more to reveng theis ronges, seeing wee have suffered such unsupportable spight.

Breck. They say I must not speake my mynd, and if I had spake it sooner, I had not byn in this case. you talke of Revenge, and I knowe not what, wee had more neede thinke how wee should mende what is amisse, and if you should have done, as I would have had you, wee should never have come to this.

2387 on Query 'of' 2408 not Query 'now'

Nifle. what Mr Brecknock, doe you begin to yeild? this is it they expect; no, no, followe our proceedings in Complayning to the Duke, and though in the beginning wee indure some smart, yet you shall see what profitt it will bringe us in the end.

Breck. I, I great proffit indeed to undoe us all and emptie our Cofers in our Chambers, great proffit I promise you.

Nifle. How now are you so lustie, doe you not consider hoe I am?

Brek. yes, yes, I doe consider what I was.

Nifle. I, I, the Towne gat much by you.

Breck. Nea, if you urge mee so farre; I say, I am sure All good men will saye, I have Carried my selfe better in my Burgomastershipp then you for all your great braggs; I left the Chist full, which you will bring to a lowe ebbe, and you must be laid in the Jaile for I knowe not what, and there spend what you list, and the Towne must beare your charges.

Nifle. I say unto thee, thou art an Asse, an a ffoole to use no better termes to him, that is your soveraine; I saye unto thee, thou art a very knowne Asse, therefore be silent and followe our proceedings in Complayning to the Duke.

Breck. ffollow you, alas I cannot, such a foole as I must have nothing to doe with wise men, hee that hath byn Mr Burgomaster twise before you hee is an Asse with you. god [keepe] me such an Asse still; I have

2437 Complayning MS. 'Complaying'

byn Called many a bad name but never asse before in all my life.

Nifle. Come, The foole runnes rashly on, then you will not assist us ?

Breck. No, no, when I ride or goe a foote further to spend one penny more in this enterprise, Ile give you leave to hange mee. take an Asses counsell and lett us recover our old estate and never seeke further.

Nifle. This is strange, that you should be so backward which have byn so forward in tymes past.

Breck. It is | strange to you that many ritch wedowes p. 59
to become Gentlewomen, but it is not so with us that live by our marchandice, being such as cheifely belong unto them. I tell you in playne termes, I must either gett my estate againe, or I cannot live here.

Nifle. well, well Brecknocke such fearefull fellowes as you are, will be the overthrow of our estate.

Breck. No, no, I will render up my freedome, for unlesse you will yeild unto it, I am gone, I cannot staye here, doe as you will, I am gone, I am gone.

Nifle. Doe you not see Mr Spruce what a teephe Asse this is ? This is good that a must use such Cowardlie Companions. what thinke you ?

Spruce. I am no body, but for myne owne part sir, you may use your discretion.

Nifle. Here comes 2. I hope will be in a better mynde. (*Enter Rumford and Coleby.*)

Rumf. what is thy horse well shod ? will hee runne

2455 to Query 'do' unless 'to' as in l. 203 = 'too.'
2464 teephe Query 'touphe' (tough)

vary well? ffaith Ise try what myne can doe, Ise putt him tote.

Cole. If you will lead the waye, myne will followe, but here is Mr Burgomaster, wee must speake with him.

Rumf. what a deele man, shall wee staye so longe? Come Mr Burgomaster wee be goeing to the Duke to complayne, faith lett us knowe your mynde quickly.

Cole. I hope wee shall spoyle the sport shortly.

Nifle. I am glad some of you have the courage. I have spoken with Brecknocke, and the Asse tells mee hee will not medle, and that hee hath medled too much alreadye. praye you Sir, take your places, that wee may the better Consult of this matter.

Rumf. Gods nayles what a foule is that, the de'ele take mee, if I did not thinke hee would alwayes prove a cowardly Lurdaine, hee did so wake when hee went to cuffing.

Coleby. ôh that every man were of my mynde, wee would hold it out.

Rumf. what a plague doe wee staye? By my saule I longe to be on my bonny naggs backe, for he is bridled and sadled all this tyme. Come billie Coleby.

Colebye. Nea, first lett us consult with Mr Burgomaster.

Rumf. why what a deele makes matter? praye the come, letts gange. but here coms the foule cart with a Lurdan like himselfe, Ile see and heele say so mickle to my face.

(*Enter Brecknock with* 2. *Burgesses.*)

2497 but here MS. 'be pere' cart Query 'carl' or 'carion' Cp. 2542.

Nifle. Hoe Mr Brecknocke is your mynde altered, I hope you will not singe your old songe.

Breck. Alter mee no alters. I am settled downe, and will not be removed, and so are all the towne unlesse | it be 2. or 3. madd headed fellowes, that care p. 60
[neither] for your good nor their owne.

Rumford. what a gods name must thou be showne?

Coleby. I such fearefull fellowes will be the spoile of us, and they crye out upon us, for the paynes wee take for the common good.

Burgesses. Nea, Mr Coleby, you goe not the right waye to worke it; if it be as Mr Brecknocke certifieth mee, wee are not able to hold our estates, you that are rich may, but wee cannot.

Nifle. yett if wee joyne togither wee may and can and shall.

Cipher. Nea, nea, I cannot tell.

Rumf. what man, what a deele shall wee doe with sick fellowes as can doe us no good? I tell thee I have 20^{li} in my purse, I and faith Ile spend it to a grey groate. but Coleby, why stand wee here so longe?

Nifle. Ah, that all my subjects were of my mynde, but Mr Rumford, you had best stay to see, if any of them can be drawne to backe our good motions.

Breck. Nea, nea, I have byn burnt already, Ile not putt my finger into the fier againe. backe that backe will, for Brecknocke.

Cipher. No, no, nor I.

2 *Burg.* Noe, not wee alone, but all the Com-

minaltie being pincht with the want of that wee had before, doe vowe and protest, that unles some order be taken, they will seeke by all meanes possible to be their servants.

Coleby. why, what meane you to shewe your selves such Cowards? why Rumford? Noe body else will. in my opinion, wee have small reason to spend our tyme, when they shall reape the Commoditie of it.

Rumf. what now Colebie? will you turne Caponer too? then the deele take you all for a Companie of great foule Carions. iffaith, Ise gange alone. for iffaith, Ise not be silke a gooscap. Ise tell sicke a tale, Ise make the towne ringe all out.

Breck. I, you will doe much.

Ciph. No, no, hee cannot.

(*They cry within* Weele keepe you from undoeing us all. it is pittie such a Butcher shoud be a headsman.)

Rumf. By my saule, and if I drawe my whyniard out of my scabbard, Ise make some of you more quiett. what a deele, will you breake my Cragg a sunder?

2 *Burgesses.* Nea, Mr Rumford, what doe you meane to make your selfe so odious? if you be not more
p. 61 reasonable they will pull | out your throate.

Rumf. pull and hange and doe what a dare you all can, all shall not helpe; for Ise either spend all, or else be revenged on their Jacks.

Nifle. Nea, Mr Rumford, doe but heare mee speake.

Rumf. Nea, Jesus blesse mee, thouse for all thy braggs turne Caponer now too.

Nifle. Nea, Mr Rumford, you be too impatient, doe but heare mee, I praye you my masters sitt downe. (*They sitt downe*).

Breck. Nea, I had as liefe stand unles you were more reasonable.

Nifle. Come, come, Ile please you all. you know all of you, how fortunate and forward I have byn of the Comon benefite; if I have not surpassed all, I am sure I have gone as farre as any in good goverment, and though I have byn Crost in my good proceedings, yett towne in regard of my duetie, might have byn bondslaves, the whole generacion of Nifles; but seeing I have not beene fortunate, I must in regard of my selfe, scorne such basenes, but for your sakes yeild my selfe. Nifle I saye must yeild himselfe for the Common good; therefore lett this be spoken, and lett it be spoken but once and without Contradiction, because I have spoke it. I thinke it good and necessary for the Common good, that both I and also wee, though it be somewhat repugnant to our estats, to myne especially being as I am, to make shewe of submission to theis gentle Athenians, shewe I saye, mistake mee not, I saye not indeed, but in shewe, so that wee may recover our estate, and then staye and meditate upon revenge untill wee may take some occasion to overthrowe them horse and man, which if wee can but take, you shall

2573 yett etc. The passage is difficult to emend.

see with what resolution I will persecute it, how saye you, my Masters? how like you the words which I have spoken?

Breck. I had rather present league were concluded, but yet I hold to this, hoping it will drawe on a greater.

Nifle. How say you Mr Rumford?

Rumf. Marry, I knowe not how to deale with lads, but Ile be no looser; I am sure some of them are in books 200^{li}. for flesh. Marry then goe you out, yet, doe what you will, Ile not see it.

2 *Burg.* what if they should putt us to our othes to yeild true obedience?

Nifle. Oathes are but words, neither doe I thinke it necessarie to stande upon strickt termes, being as it p. 62 is, but a constrayned | oath. you therefore Masters take the paynes to goe to Mr Rector, and certifie him how lies you the Cause, it grieves mee to utter it, in the meane tyme, lett us heare the supplication drawne against they come. Mr Spruce, lett us see your skill?

(*Exeunt Burgesses.*)

Spruce. As I am but one of you all, so I will not be offencible to you all.

Nifle. And so you are an Asse. Sir, art fitt to be in such a place? but least you should saye it is my doeing, you shall every one give his sentence. Begin you Mr Brecknocke.

Breck. It may be I shall prove an Asse too, but

2589 persecute Cp. note on 2382.
2596 in Query 'in my'
2605 lies MS. 'hee'
2606 heare Query 'have'

all is one; if I should drawe it, thus it should be; Lamentable reverence of this societie.

Spruce. ôh that is according to forme.

Rumf. ffy Mr Brecknock, fy, thous alwayes absurd, come, come, Mr Spruce, sett it downe and wright; wee praye, not because wees poore, but because wees fayne live in quietnesse, and be friends.

Colebye. Nea, if wee goe this waye to worke, wee must come in more humble manner, therefore it may be thus; though lamentably wee doe not complayne, yet earnestly wee intreate.

Spruce. Lamentably and earnestly agree well togither, it will be very well accepted.

Niphle. Thou alwayes bablest Spruce, hold thy peace, wilt thou give thy Judgment upon thyne owne head? I saye unto thee hould thy peace, Ile save your labour in drawing it. Ile utter it in most ample forme.

ACTUS 5us. Scena 4^{a}.

Enter Musonius, Philenius, 2 *Burgesses and the rest.*

Muson. Nowe Philenius, shall wee obtayne our whole desires? but my masters, certifye your followers, that wee here staye for them, and will take the place.

Burgesses. Here are a couple of gentle Athenians, that Mr Rector hath sent according to your direction, they have received from.

2618 is Query 'is not' 2629 *Niphle* MS. 'Niple'
2636 followers Query 'fellowes'
2640 received from The sentence is incomplete.

Niphle. well.

Burgesses. wee staye upon your worships.

Rumford. Marry and hee sad staye, and hee be ruld by mee.

Ciph. They should indeed.

Nifle. But against our wills wee must pretende some shewe of submission.

Ciph. your worshipp saith well, wee must indeed.

Muso. Sirra Philenius, take as grave a Countenance
p. 63 as thou canst. Niphle | will hardly stoope to doe us reverence.

Phile. Ile warrant thee for a Countenance, but thou shalt be Chiefe speaker man, thou art the wisest.

Muso. Ile warrant thee, wee are both wise enough, weele fitt them for a paire of—

Coleby. what must wee stande here bare headed?

Cyph. No, no, by no meanes.

Breck. wee must being in petition. doe you not knowe last yeare, when I was Burgomaster Sir Obedus Tuck stood bare headed to mee? much more must wee.

Cipher. Much more by all meanes.

Nifle. Mr Cipher you speake contradictions.

Ciph. So belike sir.

Nifle. you are an Asse sir, if wee had no wiser men then you, wee should make proper meetings of it, hold your peace, hinder not my meditations.

Cipher. you may say your pleasure now, but it is

2653 speaker MS. 'speakes'

well knowne, that I was a worthy governour in my goverment, when you were a litle boye and carried your mothers Tallies after her.

Nifle. well wee must give an Asse leave to speake, but I injoyne you silence.

Muso. mee thinkes they are very longe. Nifle is meditatinge some ffustian speech.

Phile. Like enough, but I must saye or doe something, whereby I may shewe my selfe to be in some authoritie. well Ile bid him put on his hatt.

Muso. Prethee doe, but doe [it] with a grace.

Phile. with a better Ile warrant thee then Cipher makes a legg.

Muso. ôh hee is a notable Asse, and hee will saye nothing all the daye but, yea : indeed : it is even so : by all meanes : or by no meanes : true : right : good : well.

Phile. And hot spurd Rumford, hee begins or ends every speech, with well said : breake their cragg : stricke their teeth into their throats : deele ha my saul : wack her wele.

Muso. And Nifle hele doe any thing as hee is Nicolas Nifle ; and all his fellow bretheren are Asses ; wee ragtailes.

Phile. There is a goodly rable of them, take them up roundly.

Nifle. Now, I am prepared for them.

Breck. But be not peremptory with them.

2672 well MS. 'weele'

Nifle. you shall teach mee, shall you? Come letts goe, are theis they?

2 *Burg.* I sir.

p. 64 *Nifle.* Gentlemen, | god save you, wee be come to acknowledg our errors and crave your favours.

Rumf. Gods sides hee beggs like a Coward.

Muso. nowe wee must froune on them Philenius. How comes it, that you, who have vowed your selves professed enemies against us should now in a submissive manner crave a pârlee?

Phile. Be covered Mr Nifle.

Nifle. I being chiefe of the rest will speake for the rest.

Muso. Notary, make an Act of that they saye.

Nifle. This is the thinge; seeing some discontentments, some dissentions, some warrs have passed you and us, the reason I knowe not, but as farre as I knowe, altogither from our selves. But you are termed gentle, therefore doe but consider, that it was but superioritie, for which wee doe contend, the desire whereof yee knowe (that be schollers) to be common to all beasts, which seeing it is so, wee hope, that it is pardonable. wee crave pardon, and craving pardon wee tender our supplication, that it may please you, to letts live by you, and recover our old estats, that is, to reape what benefits wee may by you, which if it please you to graunt, I being the mouth of the rest doe promise for the rest hereafter to be obedient to you in

2712 the MS. 'tha'

any reasonable demaund. how saye you my masters, have I not spoken according to your myndes?

All. you have, you have.

Muso. what Mr Nifle, is it not high tyme nowe to leave this follye, this arrogant sottishnes, this humerous surquedrye with which they use to affright weake witts?

Cipher. your worship saith true.

Muso. wee for our parts, as wee are impatient of injuries, so wee are apt to receive any submissive duetie.

Phile. nea, they are not worthy of our favours, who being in their greatest triumph, when to us they are most serviceable, yett dares presume to violate Minervaes maidenhead, and tare from her head those sacred headbands wherewith antiquitie hath honered her.

Breck. nea, good Gentlemen, pardon us, wee knowe our selves to be faultie.

Rumf. Thou alwayes bablest Brecknocke, our Burgomaster will make his matter better then thee effaith.

Nifle. I saye sir, what is past is past, and what is to come I knowe | not. p. 65

Phile. Take him downe.

Muso. Know thy selfe what thou art, thinke thy selfe no kinge because thou hast almost witt enough to be Mr Burgomaster. this arrogant humor ill befitts thy deserts, and learne to measure students, not by thy puffie apprehension, but according to their owne excellency, and know that learning and the Arts are divine, they fetch their pedigree from the high heavens. Jove himselfe had three of his ofspringe Schollers, and great Monarchs have triumphed more in their knowledg, then in their empire, and have thought them selves happy in philosophers familiarity, And will you base drudges springing from dunghills contend for superioritie?

Phile. I, I, what will they not have out of theis forgeries of villanies?

Breck. ffollowe it, follow it, they begin to fall off.

Niphle. what hath byn I know not, but hereafter I promise to be answerable to your desires, so you use mee like a magistrate.

Muso. But trust you wee dare not, being of your selves so variable, therefore how shall wee worke with you? sweare true obedience and service.

All. wee will.

Phile. notarie sett downe they will sweare.

Muso. If you doe performe it, though you have deserved all rigour, yett pittying your estats, wee will see you recover the priviledges you obtained before.

All. wee be much bound unto you.

Muso. as you carry your selves, so shall you gaine our favours; now Philenius, seeing our successe hath byn correspondent to our desires, I hope wee have performed our promises and [satisfied] our spectators.

Phile. Lett us Musonius referre that to those that

2757 had three of his ofspringe Schollers, MS. 'had there of his ofspringe. Schollers'

2779 Philenius MS. 'Philenus'

come after, and lett us now goe in, to perfect our obedience, then Gentlemen will favour us, if it be but for affection they beare Athens.

Muso. Come Sir follow us to take your oathes.

Niphle. wee follow, wee follow, Nifle must stoope, must followe.

Muso. Sirra, have wee not conjured this matter well?

Philenius. Yett passing well.

finis Act 5. *Scena* 4.

ACTUS 5us. Scena 5^a^. p. 66

Enter Tavie solus.

Tavie. Vas there ere a fine honest Shentleman vas want a callant and proper man, can keepe a horse well, a hound, or fare cood honest hore? Tavie can too it ferrie well, cod be prassed and plessed for it. vas none take her up, Cots plud vas her not in a fine taking? vas no more shefe Sargeant. 2. Shentlmen her prave lye and tale and saye Tavie was false knave and betraye Mr Burgomaster, her arship was betwene her and take her Mase from her, but marke her now, cood honest kint sister Luce put in a Cart and make her shurney out towne, and so take her leave, so Tavie lost all her custome, her fitteling put towne, no more coot Methig-

2800–1 her prave lye Query 'her make prave lye'

ling, vas become ferrie poore pegger: put her shall tell such a pawdy tale of Mr Burgomaster vas make her heare rise of her head, as Christ shall helpe her, her vas fery foole to forsake her old Master, but her comes a small Shentleman, will see and her arship will entertaine her. (*Enter Crickett.*)

Crick. God and good fortune doth still favour us, lett mee dye presently and be overwhelmed in this sea of joyes. I sawe the swyny snowts sweare true service and obedience. who would ever have thought I should have lived to see this golden Age? And was not Crickett a cheife Capteine in this action?

Tavie. Cote plesse and keepe her arship, her vas crave her cood will.

Crick. Nea, you welsh rogue, are not you packt out of the towne with kinde Luce? But saye why wouldst thou have my worships good will?

Tavie. Her vad crave to be her arships true man and servant.

Crick. Hange thee villaine, what service canst thou doe?

Tavie. Make her shamber, vipe her bed, sweepe her shoes, any thing what please.

Crick. I want no man, especially of thy making, but, vassall, thy case is pittifull, though thou deservest no pittie, yet Ile vouchsafe to speake to the Butler to make thee under skinker in the Buttery. how sayest thou knave?

p. 67 *Tavy.* Marry | cot be prassed and plessed for it, her vas thanke her arshipp ferie hartily, her vas never forsake her old Master but her shall attende upon her arship.

Crick. No sirra, goe before, and Ile come after.

Tavie. Now Shentlemen, cote be with you, and forgive her, and I pray speake well of cood honest Tavie, and honest Luce, and say Tavie was no pawde, Luce no drab, this is all her crave. (*Exit.*)

Cricket. Be gone you slave. Ile doe nothing but mocke him, Ile make him an arrant foole.

Now deere Gentlemen, I am sure you expect our returne from Athens, weele make a short cutt and satisfie your expectation. you have true Clemencie in her diverse formes. you have seene what have hapned to the hobbenoles; if you looke what is befalne to their wives, wee for our parts are carelesse what betide them. Lett them rangle with their heads, scratch out their eyes, use all rayling termes with their husbands, it shall be most acceptable newes unto us, for in their discontent rest our contentment. But if there be any such kind harted Gentlemen as are loth the poore wenches should live in misery, for their sakes, Ile take upon mee to make the attonment, trust mee I can doe it and within this halfe houre I make them friendes in a cupp of wine. As for Luce shee is gone, but I will not tell you whether, least some wenching fellow sneake after her. Now Gentlemen, I hope I have satisfied you in theis things. yet I am most afraid least in Antiquity you should seeke for our historie; will you know where it is? Turne Herodotus, and one of his 9. Muses will tell you strange newes of our Clubb lawe; but as I remember, there is an old manuscript of Thucidides, which I read but once, maks great mention of it; but to be short, you shall finde in Plato de legibus, where Plato amonge other lawes repeateth, that the Athenian Comonwealth was alwayes best governed by Clubb lawe; as for other matters I hope you will not be so severe Censurers, as to thinke in such a subject, wee can observe Commike rules, neither was it our Authors intent. ffavour our silly stage fraught with well meaning and yong Actors, and let us not want your goodwills, with having striven so much to sett out your excellency. for your sakes kind Gentlemen some of our company have shed their bloud and have thought it well shed for your sakes. many crounes wee cract this day, many bruses, many wounds for you were given and taken,

which woundes no balme can salve, no cunning hands can heale,
unlesse your gratious hands, send forth a merry peale.

(*plaudite.*)

ffinis.

CHANGES OF PUNCTUATION.

('n.s.'=no stop.)

9 wench, MS. n.s.
11 holesome? MS. 'holesome.'
17 her. and MS. n.s.
Burgomaster, MS. n.s.
18 will, will MS. n.s.
Shergeant? MS. Shergeant.
21 Commaund? MS. n.s.
22 wench, MS. n.s.
44 office. MS. n.s.
86 thing MS. 'thing,'
108 sir, MS. n.s.
123 things. MS. n.s.
129–30 villaine; MS. n.s.
140 breched, MS. n.s.
144 no, MS. n.s.
145 towne. MS. n.s.
154 away MS. 'away)'
164 are, MS. n.s.
169 doe, MS. n.s.
186 mould. MS. 'mould,'
221 us, MS. n.s.
223 Burgomaster. MS. n.s.
230 their owne MS. 'their. owne'
236 on, MS. n.s.
471 hee. MS. n.s.
505 knave), MS. n.s.
533 shewe MS. 'shewe,'
537 Cittisens. MS. n.s.
550 all, MS. n.s.
578 tell? MS. 'tell.'
580 fittle? MS. 'fittle,'
586 why? MS. 'why.'
589 two, MS. n.s.
592 pox MS. 'pox,'
593 to her? MS. 'to her,'
609 I, I, MS. 'I, I'
way, MS. n.s.
631 with you, . MS. n.s.
634 cape? MS. 'cape.'
637 Cape? MS. 'Cape.'
638 here. MS. n.s.
640 dinner? MS. n.s.
642 goe. MS. 'goe?'
650 shere, MS. n.s.
653 Cordileere, MS. n.s.
657 merry, MS. n.s.
714 two. MS. n.s.
719 Corne, MS. n.s.
745 tester, MS. n.s.
sixpence, MS. n.s.
Ribans? MS. 'Ribans.'
791 gone? MS. 'gone,'
797 her tale, MS. n.s.
802 Chamber. MS. n.s.
816 be? MS. 'be.'
830 so? MS. 'so,'
836 selfe. MS. n.s.
845 Gentleman, MS. n.s.
851 Burgomaster? MS. 'Burgomaster.'
880 wee two? MS. 'wee two.'
928 thou. MS. 'thou,'
933 us. MS. n.s.
970 incontinencye, MS. n.s.
992 shoulders. MS. n.s.
1002 pretily MS. 'pretily.'
1030 imployed, MS. n.s.
1037 Drome? MS. 'Drome.'

1038 cannot, MS. n.s.
1041 this, MS. n.s.
1046 say, MS. n.s.
1051 cleare? MS. 'cleare,'
1095 come? MS. n,s.
1112 no, MS. n.s.
1139 fellowes, MS. n.s.
1170 arrand. MS. n.s.
1175 done? MS. 'done.'
1241 speeches? MS. 'speeches.'
1251 not. MS. n.s.
1267 thing, MS. n.s.
1282 part, MS. n.s.
1286 night? MS. 'night,'
1288 watchword? MS. 'watchword,'
burne. MS. 'burne,'
1334 head, MS. n.s.
1342 intreat. MS. 'intreat,'
1343 so? MS. 'so,'
1344 friend, MS. n.s.
pate, MS. n.s.
1352 scrupulous? MS. n.s.
1368 now MS. 'now.'
1388 I, MS. n.s.
1396 well. MS. n.s.
1493 honestie. MS. 'honestie,'
1535 to, MS. n.s.
1550 heeles, MS. n.s.
1568 him, MS. n.s.
1611 kindred? MS. 'kindred,'
1620 angree, MS. n.s.
1631 dreame, MS. 'dreame.'
1642 ashamed? MS. 'ashamed.'
1647 hattbond? MS. 'hattbond.'
1674 alone, MS. n.s.
1677 vengance, MS. n.s.
1680 houses? MS. 'houses.'
1686 followe. MS. 'followe,'
1791 to, MS. n.s.
1802 doe it, MS. n.s.
1816 other, MS. n.s.
1825 matter? MS. 'matter.'
1850 faith, MS. 'faith.'
1867 soone. MS. 'soone,'
1868 Gentlemen. MS. 'Gentlemen,'
1871 Musonius. MS. 'Musonius,'
1879 humilitie. MS. n.s.
1882 passion. MS. 'passion,'
1887 one? MS. 'one,'
1890 night? MS. 'night:'
1906 indeed? MS. 'indeed,'
1909 it, MS. n.s.
1911 promise. MS. n.s.
1922 us. MS. 'us,'
1943 is, MS. n.s.
1947 Athenians, MS. n.s.
1950 Lieutenant? MS. n.s.
knave! MS. n.s.
1955 humble, MS. n.s.
1978 lustie, MS. n.s.
1989 soundly; MS. 'soundly,'
1994 abroad? MS. 'abroad.'
1998 Doe, MS. n.s.
2009 us, MS. n.s.
2023 knaves. MS. n.s.
2024 well. MS. 'well,'
2027 knocks, MS. 'knocks?'
2050 vench? MS. n.s.
2052 Gentleman. MS. 'Gentleman,'
2088 liest, MS. n.s.
2137 concert? MS. 'concert.'
2190 too? MS. 'too.'
2198 stronge? MS. 'stronge.'
2200 taking? MS. 'taking,'
2201 knaves, MS. n.s.
2203 matter, MS. n.s.
2204 wife, MS. n.s.
2215 you, MS. n.s.
2216 quiett, MS. n.s.
2257 mee MS. 'mee,'
2309 here? MS. 'here,'
2394 you? MS. 'you.'
2404 cause. MS. 'cause,'
2449 mee. MS. 'mee,'
2457 them. MS. 'them,'
2466 you? MS. 'you.'

2475 Burgomaster, MS. n.s.
2483 alreadye. MS. 'alreadye,'
2489 mynde, MS. n.s.
2496 matter? MS. 'matter,'
2497 gange. MS. n.s.
2519 good? MS. 'good.'
2521 groate. MS. 'groate,'
2550 saule, MS. n.s.
2552 quiett. MS. 'quiett,'
2558 can, MS. n.s.
2597 out, MS. n.s.
2630 Judgment MS. 'Judgment,'
head? MS. 'head,'
2634 *Philenius*, MS. n.s.
2653 man, MS. n.s.
2660 mee? MS. 'mee,'
2706 parlee? MS. 'parlee.'
2797 hore? MS. 'hore.'
2798 well, MS. n.s.
2799 up? MS. n.s.
taking? MS. 'taking,'
2880 day, MS. n.s.

NOTES.

1—4. It is not clear who is the speaker of these lines, if it is not one of the sergeants. The first words suggest that something—perhaps an attack with clubs on the University made by the town—is to take place on May Day. Scene 5, however, gives us the election of Burgomaster, and the mayoral election at Cambridge took place at Michaelmas. Perhaps 'may day' is used in the general sense of 'festivity,' 'jollification.' The allusion to the coming of the broom-man is also obscure, as there is no further reference to such a person in the play.

3. *the brome man.* The *N.E.D.* defines 'broom-man' as 'one who uses a broom, a street-sweeper,' and the later quotations there given clearly support that sense. The word seems, however, to have also denoted 'a seller of brooms.' Thus in *The London Chaunticleers*, London, 1659 (perhaps written by 1636 or earlier—printed in Hazlitt-Dodsley, XII.) one of the characters is 'Heath, a broom-man' who comes in crying 'Brooms! maids, brooms! old boots or shoes! come buy my brooms!' In Scene 4, when in disguise he says: 'I am perfectly changed: I never knew Heath the broom-man or the price of a besom, never traffick'd with maids o' th' kitchen or shopboys for old boots and shoes.' Which meaning we are to give the word in other cases is doubtful, for instance in Greene's *Upstart Courtier* (1592): 'Then Conscience was not a broom-man in Kent Street but a Courtier'; and in J. Cook's *City-Gallant* (Hazlitt-Dodsley, XI. 225): 'I should never be ashamed to call thee sister, though thou shouldst marry a broom-man.' In the passage before us the sense 'seller of brooms' seems more likely. Possibly the broom-handles were to be used as clubs.

6. *Niphill.* The pronunciation is shown by the forms 'Niphle' (477 etc.), 'Nifle' (828 etc.). The word 'nyfles' in the sense 'mockeries, pretences, literally, sniffings' (Skeat) is found in Chaucer's *Somnours Tale*, l. 52: 'He served hem with nyfles and with fables.' The *Century Dictionary* assigns to the verb 'niffle' the senses (1) 'sniffle,' 'snivel,' (2) Provincial, 'to eat hastily,' 'to steal,' 'pilfer.'

9. *bounching*, bouncing. Cp. Shaks. *M.N.D.* II. I. 70: 'the bouncing Amazon'; *Returne from Parnassus*, Pt. II. l. 1528: 'three bounsing wenches.' For the form 'bounching,' cp. 'anchestors,' l. 351 below and 'lanching' *Returne from Parnassus*, II. 95: 'where nought but lanching can the wound auayle.'

a smoker. The *English Dialect Dictionary* gives various quasi-slang uses of 'smoker' from Lancashire, East Anglia and Devonshire, *e.g.* as applied to a rain-storm, 'Here comes an old smoker,' or to the devil, 'The old smoker take the pig,' or to an improbable story, 'What a smoker!'

10. *turne.* Perhaps for 'turned' (cp. l. 1996), but the sense is not clear. Cp. l. 1087, etc. Possibly there should be a comma after 'her,' and the next words mean '[who] is never taught [to say] no forsooth.' Tavie uses 'as' to mean 'is' (l. 34). Cp. Shirley, *Lady of Pleasure* (1637), II. 1: 'What luck did I not send him into France! They would have...taught him...to talk not modestly, Like "ay forsooth" and "no forsooth"; to blush, And look so like a chaplain!'

22. *prance.* This may be a variant form of the adj. 'prank' found in *Lingua*, IV. 7. 94: 'If I do not seem pranker now, then I did in those days.' The verbal forms 'prance' and 'prank' are said by Skeat to be closely allied. On the other hand, when we have corruptions in this text like 'intraunt' for 'in trot' (l. 650, etc.), one may well take 'prance' here to be a mere corruption of 'prave,' Tavie's form of 'brave.'

23. *plesed*, *i.e.* blessed. Cp. l. 1268 'plessed.'

28. *Clubb lawe.* The term 'club-law' ('the use of the club to enforce obedience, physical force as contrasted with argument,' etc.) seems not to be found before the date of this play. The *N.E.D.* has an example under 1612 from T. Taylor's *Comm. Titus* (ed. 1619), I. 7: 'The castle is not wonne by fists or club-law.' We hear earlier, however, of apprentices or students raising their fellows to take their part in some commotion by the cry 'Clubs.' Cp. *Introduction*, pp. xvi, xviii, and *Three Lords and Three Ladies of London* (1590) (Hazlitt-Dodsley, VI. 459), '*stage direction: Simplicity makes a great noise within, and enter with three or four weaponed. Simplicity*: Clubs! Clubs!... I charge ye 'prehend them.' Cp. Addison, *Spectator*, IX.: 'When our universities found there was no end of wrangling this way [*i.e.* by syllogism] they invented a kind of argument which is not reducible to any mood or figure in Aristotle. It was called the Argumentum Basilinum (others write it Bacilinum or Baculinum) which is pretty well expressed in our English word club-law. When they were not able to confute their antagonist they knocked him down. It was their method in their polemical debates, first to discharge their syllogisms, and afterwards to betake themselves to their clubs, until such time as they had one way or other confounded their gainsayers.'

46. *god send you good shipping*, God prosper you. Mr McKerrow refers me to Kyd's *Soliman and Perseda*, IV. 2. 79: 'Farewell, counterfeite foole, God send him good shipping'; and Nashe's *Unfortunate Traveller* (*Wks.* ed. McKerrow, II. 222. 26): 'Gone he is; God send him good shipping to Wapping.' Mr McKerrow remarks that in both these cases the phrase

is used somewhat ironically, as one might say 'The devil go with him,' and that in the second case the words 'to Wapping' seem part of the fixed phrase, as the person was not apparently going to Wapping, nor indeed to sea at all. Whether in our play the phrase has an ironical colouring is an open question.

66. *Puffe.* There is a character 'Captain Puff' in *Ram Alley.*

67. *such a long fellow.* Apparently Mr Rumford, as Puff is called 'the fat sergeant.' Cp. ll. 94, 157, 158.

75. *Cricket.* The name perhaps suggested 'a merry fellow.' See *Introduction*, p. liii, and cp. *Ralph Roister Doister* (Hazlitt-Dodsley, III. 82): 'He bet the King of Crickets (? = the Lord of Misrule) on Christmas Day That he....' In the Prologue to the *Returne from Parnassus*, Pt. II. Momus is addressed by the Defender of the play 'thou scurvie Jack,' 'you paultry Crittick.' For the last word the MS. has 'crickhett.' Possibly the other reading is to be preferred, but the corruption is suggestive.

94. *riprapp*, a rap, knock, continued knocking. Cp. ll. 1290, 1947. The compound in this sense is not in the *Century Dictionary.* Cp. however *Thersites* (Hazlitt-Dodsley, I. 428): 'She knappeth me in the nose With rip, rap, Flip, flap.'

96. *gave me such a...fall.* Cp. l. 271. Cp. *Lusty Juventus*: '*Hipocrisye.* I set up great ydolatry...To geve mankind a fall'; *Hycke Scorner*: '*Frewyll.* I have a noble here. Who lente it me? By Cryste, a frere, And I gave hym a fall'; *New Custom* (Hazlitt-Dodsley, III. 38): 'First I would buffet him thus, then give him a fall.'

97. *bobies*, simpletons. Cp. ll. 1656, 2139, 2152. The earliest quotation in the *N.E.D.* is from *Patient Grissel* (1599—1603).

99. *As take her lodging*, he has taken refuge in college. Cp. ll. 595, 2325.

102. *unles* = lest. The *Imperial Dictionary* quotes R. Greene: 'Beware you do not once the same gainsay, Unless with death he do your rashness pay.'

115. *the hall.* Apparently this means 'the college,' which is generally in the play called 'lodgings.' Cricket had been pursued by the Sergeants, including of course Tavie.

that we might but had. For the omission of 'have' before the past participle, cp. Kyd, *Spanish Tragedy*, III. 3. 41: 'Come sir you had been better kept your bed Than have committed this misdeed so late.'

116. *skulls punishment.* I have found no other example of this phrase. One might consider 'skulls' a corruption of 'raskalls,' or a proper name: but the phrase is intelligible as it stands.

118. *buy...a Scottish dagger.* Cp. l. 1389. The dagger or dirk was a regular part of a Highlander's equipment. John Major, writing in 1512, says that the Highlanders carry a large dagger, sharpened on one side only, but very sharp, under the belt (J. Anderson, *Ancient Scottish Weapons*, 1881, p. 21).

Scottish daggers or *quhingars* 'bravelie and maist artificiallie made and embroiderit with gold' appear as gifts from Mary Queen of Scots and the King, to the French Ambassador in 1566 (Fairholt, *Costume in England*, II. 144).

123. *By the masse.* Cp. l. 1806: 'By the messe.'

125. *gravities*, persons of grave deportment, persons of consideration. The *N.E.D.* quotes *Barnevelts Apol.* (1618): 'with...bending submission to your gravitie'; Prynne (1629): 'It cannot be unknown to your gravities.'

give them the cringe, *i.e.* a 'deferential obeisance' (*N.E.D.*). Cp. *Returne from Parnassus*, Pt. I. (1600), V. 3. 1562: 'Each tapster's cringe'; *Lingua* (1607), V. 3: 'with a lowly Cringe presents the Wine.'

133. *how fares your bodie?* Cp. l. 887: '*how does your bodie?*' The phrase is not in the *N.E.D.* Cp. T. Tomkin, *Albumazar* (1615), III. 7 (Hazlitt-Dodsley, XI. 368): 'How does your body, Ronca?' *Wily Beguiled* (Hawkins' *Ancient Drama*, III. 355): 'Gripe. What, master Churms?...how fares your body?'

136. *brechinge*, flogging. Cp. l. 2041. Cp. *Lingua* (1607), III. 1: 'I owe Anamnestes a breeching'; and *Two Angry Women of Abington* (1599) (Hazlitt-Dodsley, VII. 335): 'this is your boy...you must breech him for it.' Students at Cambridge were liable to corporal punishment, so long as they were undergraduates. Cp. J. W. Clark, *Riot*, etc. (*Camb. Ant. Soc. Publ.* XLIII.), p. 36: 'The stone casters to be suspended of degree yf graduates, yf noe whipped' (16$\frac{10}{11}$).

139. *Childest*, childishest. The form is not in the *N.E.D.*

144. *the sir reverence of the towne.* Cp. l. 423. Shakspeare, *Comedy of Errors*, III. 2. 90: 'What is she?—A very reverent body; ay, such a one as a man may not speak of without he say "Sir reverence."' The phrase 'sir reverence' is apparently a corruption of 'saving (or "save") your reverence.' It is often introduced by way of apology for some later words. Cp. *New Custom* (Hazlitt-Dodsley, III. 9): 'It would almost for anger (sir reverence!) make a man to piss.'

145. *Mr Brecknock...and I have had a full meete.* Cp. l. 2296. Cp. Chettle and Day, *The Blind Beggar of Bednall-Green* (Bang's *Materialien*), l. 2138: 'I had a full blow at his left leg.' Marston, *Parasitaster*, IV.: 'Stand; Herod, you are full met, Sir.' No example of 'meet' as a subs. is given in the *N.E.D.* before the 19th century.

147. *got the wall of him*, got the better of him. Cp. *Rom. and Jul.* I. 1. 15: 'I will take the wall of any man or maid.'

148. *I was for him*, I was ready to meet him. Cp. l. 1368, and Shakspeare, *T. of Shrew*, IV. 3. 152: 'I am for thee' (*i.e.* ready to fight thee).

159. *the dayntelest.* Cp. l. 1370, 'the fineliest.'

162. *come over.* From what follows I take 'come over' to be the phrase

used by a schoolmaster to a boy whom he desired to flog—though I find no authority for such a use given in the *N.E.D.* Cp. *Lingua*, III. 3 *ad fin.*: 'I learnt a trick t' other day, to bring a Boy ore the thigh finely.' This suggests that our phrase is an invitation to *come* 'ore the thigh.' Another line of the same scene of *Lingua* carries the action to its goal: 'Untrusse thy points and whip thee.'

167. *Sir boy.* Cricket's resentment at being called a boy is seen again in ll. 1203—4. Cp. Marlowe, *Faustus*, IV. 1: '*Wag.* Sirrah boy, come hither. *Clown.* How boy! swowns, boy! I hope you have seen many boys with such pickadevaunts as I have: boy, quotha!'; *Marriage of Wit and Science* (Hazlitt-Dodsley, II. 347): '*Wit.* O my sweet boy...*Will.* I pray you Sir call me your man, and not your boy'; *Three Lords and Three Ladies of London* (1590) (Hazlitt-Dodsley, VI. 387): 'good boys—be not angry that I call you boys, for ye are no men yet...and yet I have seen boys angry for being called boys. Forsooth they would be called youths.'

191. *humanity*, refinement of manners, civility. Milton, *Areopagitica*, *ad in.*: 'better to imitate the old and elegant humanity of Greece than the barbaric pride of a Hunnish...stateliness.'

196. *goe further and speed worse.* The saying is given in J. Heywood's *Proverbs* (1546): 'You...might haue gone further and haue faren wurs.'

199. *druggs.* The word in the MS. has the 's' which sometimes seems to indicate 'es.' If the word should be transcribed 'drugges' it may be merely a variant spelling of 'drudges,' the form found elsewhere in this play. Cp. *Returne from Parnassus*, Pt. I. 1337: 'shame to see thy sonns Made servile druges to the female sex.' By 'drudge,' 'drug' is however found at this period. The *N.E.D.* quotes Greene, *Disput.* (1592), 31: 'so base a drug as his mayd'; and *Timon of Athens*, IV. 3. 254.

222. *Bakerlie.* There is a special point in the application of this epithet to Niphle, see l. 462. In l. 505 it seems to be a mere term of abuse, like 'coal-carrierly' in *Wily Beguil'd* (Hawkins' *Ancient Drama*, III. 302) and 'souterly' in *Like will to Like* (Hazlitt-Dodsley, III. 321). The only example of 'bakerly' in the *N.E.D.* is taken from *Pass. Morrice* (1593), 82: 'spindle shankte or bakerly kneed.'

petifogging. Cp. l. 464. The first example of the adj. in the *N.E.D.* dates from 1603.

223. *hee hath bought him a satten sute all readie.* See *Introduction*, p. li, *bot.*

224. *have a fling at.* The phrase is used either in a hostile sense as here, and in l. 1652 (cp. Holland, *Pliny*, 1601, quoted in the *N.E.D.*: 'haue a fling at magicians for their abhominable lies'); or in the sense 'try to obtain' (implied in l. 1653). Cp. Greene, *Selimus* (before 1592), l. 2563: 'We'll haue a fling at the Ægyptian crowne'; and *Wily Beguil'd* (Hazlitt-Dodsley, IX. 244): 'If I had not a month's mind in another place, I would have a fling at her.'

234. *unconstant.* The form occurs four times in Shakspeare.

239. *Tavie bringing out Cushions.* Cp. *Coriolanus*, II. 2, *stage direction* '*Enter two* Officers, *to lay cushions* [*i.e.* before the meeting of the Senate for the choice of Consuls]'; *Lingua*, III. 2, *stage direction:* 'Mendacio *with Cushions under his arms*,' and l. 8 *inf.*: 'But Sirra whither with these Cushions? *Men.* To lay them here that the Judges may sit softly, lest my Lady *Lingua's* cause go hard with her.'

244. *soull bell*, passing-bell. The *Century Dictionary* quotes Bishop Jos. Hall, *Apol. against Brownists*, § 43: 'We call them soul-bells for that they signify the departure of the soul, not for that they help the passage of the soul.'

245. *sauce boxes*, impudent fellows. Cp. *Englishmen for my Money*, III. 2 (Hazlitt-Dodsley, x. 509): 'Why sauce-box? how now, you unreverent minx?'

247. *this geare*, this business. Cp. l. 1318.

261. *Mr Thirtens.* See *Introduction*, p. xlix.

263. *to Thebes to buy some ffells at the leather fayre.* 'Thebes' stands perhaps for London.

265. *fine Mr Thirtens, a marke, that is, a groate more then his name* (since a groat is 4*d.* and a mark 13*s.* 4*d.*). Cp. a similar pun on 'noble' (=6*s.* 8*d.*) in *Look about you* (1600) (Hazlitt-Dodsley, VII. 436): 'Thus jets my noble skink along the street, And yet my noble humour is too light By the six shillings. Here are two crack'd groats.'

271. *Jade*, a horse of a poor kind.

Mr Moone is sicke and hath a kercher, *i.e.* is unwell and hath his head bound up. Cp. *Wealth and Health* (Malone Society), 781: 'Helth commeth in with a kercher on his head.'

273. *Mr Silverburrowe.* See *Introduction*, p. xlix.

275. *mercement*, fine.

276. *Mr ffescu.* The name is taken from a *fescu*, a pointer used for pointing out letters in teaching children to read.

Mr Mallice. Possibly this name was meant to suggest Wallis, though Wallis was an Alderman and not one of the Four and Twenty.

279. *Goodman Hornesbie.* 'Goodman' was a title inferior to 'Master.' Cp. *Returne from Parnassus*, Pt. I. 722: 'the ignorant people that before calde mee *Will* nowe call mee *William*, and you of the finer sorte call mee *good man Percevall*.'

280. (*Brecknock neeseth.*) *Goosturd. Munne. Hornesby. God blesse your worship.* (I suppose that 'Munne' is the same as 'Moone.' His name is not called separately, and there are Four and Twenty without him.) On customs connected with sneezing, see Tylor, *Primitive Culture* (4th ed.), I. pp. 97—104. Tylor quotes from *Rules of Civility*, 1685 (trans. from the French): 'If his lordship chances to sneeze, you are not to bawl out "God bless you, sir."'

Mr McKerrow refers me to a pseudo-historical account of the origin of the custom in Polydore Vergil, *De invent. rerum*, VI. c. XI. (speaking of the times of Pelagius): 'Subijt aliud pestis genus, vt cum quis sternuisset aliquoties, continuo occideret: vnde mos, sicut quidam tradunt, creuit, vt audientes quempiam sternutantem illico dicerent, Te Deus adiuuet: quod hodie seruatur.'

On the form *neeseth*, see *Midsummer Night's Dream*, II. I. 56 (Mr Aldis Wright's note).

285. *Mr Westcocks.* See *Introduction*, p. xlix.

goodman Woodcocke. The use of 'woodcock' to signify 'dolt' was very common.

291. *otherwiselike.* The compound is not in the *N.E.D.*

295. *a true-penny*, a good fellow. Cp. Shaks. *Hamlet*, I. 5. 150.

314. *the Duke.* By 'the Duke' in this play we must understand 'the Queen.' In *A Midsummer Night's Dream* and in Chaucer's *Knight's Tale*, Theseus is 'Duke' of Athens.

318. *Mr Slugg.* This name again may have been suggested by that of the Town Clerk, Henry Slegg, though he was not one of the Four and Twenty.

327. *with those that wee have.* Twenty-four names have been called. This was the number of the Council or 'brethren' at Cambridge, exclusive of the Mayor and Aldermen. See *Introduction*, p. xxvii.

333. *comparisons being so odious.* The *N.E.D.* shows that this proverbial saying is found in Lydgate, *Hors, shepe & G.* (1430), 204: 'Odyous of olde been comparisons.' It occurs also in Lyly's *Euphues* (Arber), 68, in Lyly's *Midas*, IV. I *ad in.*, and in Shaks. *Much Ado*, III. 5. 18.

336. *leave theise circumprances.* The word 'circumprances,' which is not found in the *N.E.D.*, is a happy Malapropism of Mr Rumford's. He similarly uses 'prologue' in the sense 'gist, conclusion.' Cp. *Lingua*, I. 8: 'I know no danger, leave these circumstances.'

338. *time hath winges.* Cp. Shirley, *Cardinal*, II. I: 'She will think Time hath no wing, till I return'; *Traitor*, I. 2: 'when the happier things Call to enjoy, each saucy hour hath wings.'

340. *Machivillians.* The *N.E.D.* quotes from *Satir. Poems Reform* (1568): 'This false Machivilian'; and from Marston's *Pygmalion* (1598): 'A damn'd Macheuelian.'

341. *good St Mary.* The oath 'by saint Mary' is found in *Hycke-Scorner*, *New Custom* and other plays.

342. *Rector*, *i.e.* Vice-chancellor. The word is probably adopted from its use in German Universities. Cp. Marlowe, *Faustus*, II. 40 (of Wittenberg): 'let us go and inform the Rector.'

343. *nurceries*, I suppose, the colleges. *fraternities*, trade-guilds (?)

Philarches (MS. 'Philarche'). The plural seems necessary as 'Philarches'

8—2

in the University are stated to correspond to 'Bayliffs' in the town. Perhaps the Heads of Houses are meant. The word 'Phylarche' was used by More in the *Utopia*.

344. *anteambulers*. I suppose that by these the Esquire Bedells are meant. The *N.E.D.* does not give the word, though it has 'anteambulo' (1609) and 'anteambulate' (1623).

345. *nomenclators*, perhaps the officials who called over the roll or marked attendance at hall and chapel.

348. *you have parbraked your minde very well.* Cp. Hall, *Virgidemiarum*, I. 5. 9: 'when he hath parbrak'd his grieved mind.' 'Parbraked' means properly 'vomited.' Cp. Spenser, *F. Queene*, I. I. 20: 'her filthy parbreake all the place defiled has.'

349. *zemblance*, assemblance.

351. *anchestors*. See l. 9 'bounching,' *n.*

364. *adverb*. A Malapropism for 'proverb,' perhaps under the influence of 'adage.'

so many men, so many meanings. In the *Proverbs* of J. Heywood (1546), ed. Sharman, p. 14, Terence's saying 'Quot homines tot sententiae' takes the form 'so many heads, so many wits'; in the prologue to *New Custom* (Hazlitt-Dodsley, III. 6): 'many heads, many wits.' Gascoigne in his *Notes...concerning verse* quotes it in Latin, but in his *Glasse of Government* (1575) translates it by 'so many men, so many mindes.'

368. *seldome comes the better*. J. Heywood in his *Proverbs* (1546), ed. Sharman, p. 17, has 'seldome comth the better.' Cp. Chettle's *Kind-hearts Dream* in the New Shakspere Society's *Shakspere Allusion-Books*, 68. 7: 'The olde Proverbe is verefied, Seldome comes the better.' *Two Angry Women of Abington* (Hazlitt-Dodsley, VII. 302): '*Nicholas* [who speaks proverbs]: I pray God save my master's life, for seldom comes the better.' T. Heywood, *Edward IV.* Part I. I. 2: 'For as one comes, another's ta'en away; And seldom comes the better, that's all we say.'

379. *mammocks*, fragments.

382. *confiscated*. Brecknock seems to use the word loosely in the sense 'wasted,' 'ruined.'

385. *hee is non plus*. Cp. *Pilgrimage to Parnassus*, 684: 'ether saie somewhat for thy selfe or hang and be *non plus*' [with a pun on the words]; *Returne from Parnassus*, Pt. II. 1: '*Boy*. Spectators we will act a Comedy (*non plus*).'

389. *goosecape*, booby, simpleton. Cp. 2543. For the spelling, cp. l. 634 *n.*

398. *by Cocke*, a corrupted form of 'by God.' So in *Returne from Parnassus*, Pt. I. 1076. In *The Divils Charter* (Bang's *Materialien*), l. 1668, we have the oath 'Coxwounds.'

409. *I am not ashamed of my name*. So in T. Heywood, *If you know*

not me, etc., Pt. II. II. 2: 'What might we call your name?—Why, my name is John Goodfellow. I hope I am not ashamed of my name.'

420. *dea, dea*, supposed Northern English or Scotch for 'do, do.' Cp. l. 474.

423. *sir reverence.* See l. 145 *n.* Evidently an apology for the end of his sentence.

425. *made a scape*, broke wind. I do not know of any other instance of this use of the phrase. 'Scape' has often the general sense 'a fault, error': cp. Shaks. *Lucrece*, 747.

428. *goverment.* This form is found also in ll. 2571, 2670, and elsewhere. See *Introduction*, p. xxv, ll. 17, 21.

437. *fettering a wench.* I know nothing of the incident referred to.

445. *Mr Electors you were best about your dueties.* The electors apparently here retire into the Court hall. Cp. l. 466.

446. *dissemblance*, a Malapropism for 'assemblance.' Cp. l. 349. 'Dissemblance' is used in the sense 'dispersion' by Heywood, *Spider and F.* II. 33: 'assemblaunce turneth to dissemblaunce,' and in the sense 'dissimulation' by Marston, *What you will*, II. *ad fin.*: 'he that climbs a hill Must wheel about, the ladder to account Is sly dissemblance.'

447. *fect*, an aphetic form of 'effect.' Cp. the form *feckless* = 'effectless' (Shakspeare, *Tit.* III. I. 76, *Per.* V. I. 53). For similar aphetic forms, cp. l. 810, 'scuse' (=excuse) and *Narcissus* (ed. Lee), 152: 'tention' (=attention) and 425: 'minitive' (=diminutive).

458. *Mr Shavett.* See *Introduction*, p. xliv.

466. *A Niphill.* The 'a' in such combinations is not the indefinite article, but = 'ah,' 'ho.' The *N.E.D.* gives no example of the formula except as used as a war-cry (*e.g.* in *Merlin* (*c.* 1450), 'than thei cried a Clarence with a lowde voyse'). Cp. however Shirley, *Hyde Park* (1637), III. I (during a footrace): '*Within.* A Teague! a Teague! hey!'; IV. 3 (after a horse-race in which Jockey has won): '*Enter a* Bagpiper *and* Jockey *in triumph. All.* A Jockey! a Jockey!'

472. *is hee gone for?* Mr Niphle was present at the opening of the scene, and it is not clear at what point he departed.

487. *should* (*i.e.* refuse it).

492. *old men for witt, and yong men for wisdome.* As Niphle goes on to say, the terms 'old men' and 'young men' should be inverted. The ascription to Marcus Aurelius is probably made at random.

497. *muchomar.* I can make nothing of this word, and can only suggest it may be a corruption of 'wacheman.' It is not necessary to quote examples of the frequent collocation 'the constable and his watch.'

498. *timbersome*, timorous. The *Century Dictionary* has the forms 'timersome,' 'timoursome,' but not 'timbersome.' For 'timersome' cp. W. Scott, *Pirate*, XVIII.

501. *wee have byn made servants of Rulers*, *i.e.* after having been Rulers.

504. *a snipp snapp Barber*. Cp. Lyly, *Midas*, III. 2: '*Motto* (a barber): I have taught thee the knacking of the hands.' On this Mr W. H. Williams comments (*Specimens of the Elizabethan Drama*, p. 447): "To snap the fingers and the scissors with great dexterity was considered a trait of an accomplished barber. Cp. Stubbes, *Anatomie of Abuses*, 'Then snap go the fingers full bravely, God wot' (F.). Greene, *Quip for an Upstart Courtier*, addressing the barber, says 'at every word a snap with your scissors.' The barber in *The Silent Woman* (i. 1), 'has not the knack with his sheers or his fingers.' In Cooke's *Green's Tu Quoque*, 1614, sig. D 3, the barber is to be 'one that can snap his fingers with dexterity.'" Dekker and Pope use 'snip-snap' in a transferred sense. Cp. Dekker, *Old Fortunatus*, I. 1: '*Fort.* ...a pox on thee for mocking me! *Echo.* A pox on thee for mocking me! *Fort.* Why so, snip snap, this war is at an end'; Pope, *Dunciad*, II. 240: 'Dennis and dissonance and captious art And snip-snap short and interruption smart.'

505. *give him* (*the Bakerly Knave*). If the sentence is not incomplete, we may perhaps understand it to mean 'apply to him the insulting name of "Bakerly Knave."' 'Bakerly' as applied to 'Brecknock' or some other Mayor of Cambridge was probably a general term of contempt (cp. l. 222 *n.*). In Niphle's case, as he was the son of a baker (cp. l. 462) it would have had a particular reference, but Niphle cannot be here speaking of himself. A bracket seems to have been occasionally used with words which together constituted a single phrase. Cp. 'the other parte...to remayne *in* the keping of (Custos Rotulorum)' (*Boke of the justyce of paes*, *c.* 1532, fo. lxxxix.).

507. *pocketted up*. Cp. l. 1240. In this transferred sense 'pocket up' seems to occur earlier than 'pocket.'

517. *boult*, sift.

519. *horsbreade*. Cp. Hall, *Virgidemiarum*, V. 2. 97: 'When their brasse pans and winter couerled Haue wipt the maunger of the horses-bread' (*i.e.* when they are reduced to extreme poverty).

520. *the whole generacion of them*. Cp. T. Heywood, *If you know not me*, etc. II. 2: 'we are honest, all the generation of us.'

523. *out brave us in our owne dunghills*. J. Heywood, *Proverbs* (ed. J. Sharman, 1874, p. 53): 'Every cocke is proud on his owne dunghill.' The editor quotes from the *Ancren Riwle*, 'ase me seith þet coc is kene on his owne mixenne.'

525. *with bag and baggage*. The phrase is of military origin. Cp. *As you like it*, III. 2. 170: 'let us make an honourable retreat, though not with bag and baggage.'

529. *manure theise affaires*, handle, take in hand, these affairs. None of the examples of 'manure' in the *N.E.D.* are exactly parallel to this.

558. *blocks*, senseless creatures.

560. *but* (apparently superfluous). Cp. l. 1104.

567. *a murren.* Cp. *Divils Charter* (1607) (Bang's *Materialien*), 2715: 'take a murren with thee so fare-well.'

570. *tic, tac, toc* (representing his knocks on the door). Cp. *Albumazar* (1615), III. 8 (Hazlitt-Dodsley, XI. 375): 'Tick, tock, who is within here? (*Knocks on the tub.*)'

580. *fittle.* Tavie was a victualler. See *Introduction*, p. xlv.

581. *pastie and pie.* No special Welsh connotation for these words is recognized in the *N.E.D.*

591. *Nay, cover her head man.* Cricket for purposes of his own was obsequiously polite to Tavie. Cp. *Returne from Parnassus*, Pt. I. 500, where the tailor recounts a similar case: 'They came to mee, and were as curteous as passeth; I doe not like they shoulde putt of theire hatts so much to mee: well, they needs...woulde borowe 40*s.* for three dayes.'

595. *our lodging, i.e.* College. Cp. ll. 1074, 2325, etc.

603. *saucie Jacke*, impudent good-for-nothing. *prat*, prate (?).

608. *'tis too, too grosse.* Cp. l. 700. *Lingua*, I. 1 *ad fin.*: ''tis too too dangerous.' *Hamlet*, I. 2. 129: 'O that this too too solid flesh would melt.' *Returne from Parnassus*, Pt. II. Prologue 86: 'if you did not schollers blesse, Their case...were too too pittilesse.'

621. *Mounsier Grand Combatant.* The phrase was perhaps a stock one for a 'miles gloriosus.' Cp. *Ralph Roister Doister* (Hazlitt-Dodsley, III. 145): '*D. Doughty.* Down with this little quean.... *C. Custance.* I myself will mounsire grand captain undertake.' *Returne from Parnassus*, Pt. I. 352: 'Mounsier's Ajax vaine' (perhaps in allusion to this play).

622. *it would make a horse laugh to heare him talke.* Cp. Chettle and Day, *Blind Beggar of Bednall Green* (Bang's *Materialien*), 744: 'it would make a Horse break his Bridle to see the humours of these fellows.'

623. *Ile carrie him to the feast, as rounde as a Julers boxe.* There is a play on the word 'round' in its sense 'unceremoniously, promptly,' and its original sense 'circular.' Cp. P. Stubbes, *Anatomie of Abuses*, 1585 (reprint 1836, p. 140): 'to Bocardo goeth he as rounde as a ball'; and *Misogonus*, II. 4. 96 (*Quellen und Forschungen*, LXXX.): 'heile come a [? as] round as a purr' [where 'purr' probably means 'pig' as Mr McKerrow tells me].

632. *in trot.* 644. *intrant.* 650. *Intraunt.* 2020. *pie my traunt*, etc. The phrases 'in troth,' 'by my troth' in the mouths of French and Italian speakers appear regularly in the comedies as 'in trot,' 'by my trot.' Cp. *Triumphs of Love and Fortune* (1589) (Hazlitt-Dodsley, VI. 202, etc.); *Three Ladies of London* (1584) (*ibid.* VI. 273, etc.); *Englishmen for my Money* (1616) (*ibid.* X. 525); Dekker, *The Wonder of a Kingdom*, *Old Fortunatus*, etc. The forms 'intrant,' 'Intraunt' which occur here are perhaps corruptions due to a scribe.

634. *at de cape.* 636. *in de Cape.* This probably means the tavern

called the Cardinal's Cap, which stood on the site of the present Pitt Press. For the spelling cp. 'goosecape,' l. 389.

638. *Mr Burgomaster makes a great feast.* See *Introduction*, p. li.

643. *tis no madder for dat.* Cp. l. 2029 'Its [no] madder for datt,' l. 2271 'tit no matter for tut.' The sense of the three phrases is clearly the same.

651. *fleshmakers.* The word is probably meant to be bad English for 'fleshers, butchers.' It does not occur in the *N.E.D.*

653. *make good Cordileere.* A Cordelier was a Franciscan friar of the strict rule. Cp. Butler, *Hudibras*, I. I. 260: 'Of rule as sullen and severe As that of rigid Cordeliere.' Mounsier probably means that Puff is so little of an epicure that he would make a good Cordelier.

656. *Cavelero*, gentlemanlike, genteel. Dr Caius uses the word (=Chevalier) in *Merry Wives*, III. 3. 77: 'Caveleiro Slender.'

664. *it would make them disburse their Coine.* If Colby carried corn away from Cambridge, the price of that which remained would be raised and the town thereby would 'save an honest penny.' Cp. l. 1008.

668. *mount your judgment.* Does the word 'mount' here mean 'elevate' as Sylvester, *tr. of Du Bartas*, I. 7: 'that we...may mount our thoughts to heav'nly meditations'; or 'make available for use, as one mounts a cannon,' as Shaks. *King John*, II. I. 381: 'Let France and England mount Their battering cannon charged to the mouths'?

671. *hoyden*, rude, rustic. Cp. l. 817, etc. Chettle and Day, *Blind Beggar of Bednall Green* (Bang's *Materialien*), 866: a sort 'of Momes and Hoydons that know not chalk from cheese, and can talk of nothing but how they sell a score of Cow-hides at Lyn marte.' The earliest quotations for the word in the *N.E.D.* have a Cambridge connotation; Nashe, 4 *Lett. confut.* (1593), 58: 'The hoyden and pointing stock of recreation of Trinitie Hall'; *Returne from Parnassus*, Pt. I. (1600), II. I. 833.

672. *Ragge tayles, longe tayles, tatter tayles.* These soubriquets no doubt refer to the wearing of gowns, often not in the best condition. 'Ragtail' is not in the *N.E.D.* nor 'longtail' (in its University application).

680. *By my tricks*, by all I know, all the skill I have (?).

688. *poor snakes*, poor creatures. Cp. *Sir John Oldcastle*, IV. I (Hazlitt, *Doubtf. Plays of Sh.*, p. 139) (a parson is talking to Henry V. whom he takes for a common soldier): 'I'll tell thee, good fellow; we have every day tithes, offerings, christenings, weddings, burials; and you poor snakes come seldom to a booty.' Massinger, *Maid of Honour*, I. I (ed. H. Coleridge, col. 191 b foot): 'the late poor snakes our neighbours, warm'd in our bosoms.' 'Snakes' alone='wretches,' 'poor creatures' in Fletcher and Massinger, *Spanish Curate*, III. i. 23. (I am indebted for this note to Mr McKerrow.)

696. *jett it*, strut about, give themselves airs. Cp. Heywood, *Four P. P.* (Hazlitt-Dodsley, I. 384): 'should a beggar be a jetter?'; *Ralph Roister Doister* (*ibid.* III. 108): 'Then must ye stately go, jetting up and down'; *Look about*

you (1600) (*ibid.* VII. 436): 'Thus jets my noble Skink along the streets To whom each bonnet vails and all knees bend'; Shaks. *Twelfth Night*, II. 5. 36: 'how he jets under his advanced plumes!'

703. *twacke their Crags*, thwack their necks, or shoulders.

714. *nobles.* A noble was a coin worth 6*s.* 8*d.*, minted by various kings from Edward III. to Edward IV.

718. *forestall the markett.* See *Introduction*, p. xii, *n.* 1.

719. *you have obteyned your suit.* See *Introduction*, p. xlvii.

742. *more...then* 60. *headsmen* [*spend*] *in scarlet.* Cp. ll. 497, 674, 2548. The first quotation for 'headsman' in the *N.E.D.* has a Cambridge connotation: *Returne from Parnassus*, Pt. II. (1602), 1864: 'The worshipful headsmen of the towne.' The term probably covered the Mayor, Aldermen and 'Brethren' or Councillors.

shoetyings. The *Century Dictionary* (which does not give 'shoe-tying') thus defines 'shoe-tie': 'A ribbon or silk braid for fastening the two sides of a shoe together, usually more ornamental than a shoe-string, and formerly very elaborate.' Cp. N. Field, *A Woman is a Weathercock* (1612) (Hazlitt-Dodsley, XI. 30): 'Out, green shoe-strings, out! Wither in pocket since my Luce doth pout'; Jonson, *Every Man out of his Humour*, Induction, 263: 'a Rooke, in wearing...a yard of shoe-tie.' Since shoe-ties were introduced into England from France (Nares) 'Master Shooty' (*Measure for Measure*, IV. 3. 18) is the name given to a 'great traveller.'

743. *an end of a point*, an end of a tag used to fasten one's clothes.

745. *a tester*, a name given to shillings coined by Henry VIII. and to sixpences later.

746. *informe their prodigality.* Cp. *Coriolanus*, I. 6. 42: 'he did inform the truth.'

753. *tympanies.* Tympany was a kind of dropsy in which the belly was swelled out like a drum (*Century Dict.*). The word lends itself to a *double entente.*

779. *the deale on my cragge.* This is a northern form of the oath 'the devil break my (thy, etc.) neck' found in *The World and the Child* (Hazlitt-Dodsley, I. 257), *Jacob and Esau* (*ibid.* II. 190), *New Custom* (*ibid.* III. 32).

791. *plutter her nayles.* See next note. The phrase 'Gods blothernales' occurs in *Misogonus*, III. I. 195 (*Quellen und Forschungen*, LXXX.).

794. *Cotts plutt.* In the *Hundred Mery Talys* (reprint, 1866), p. 56, a Welshman swears 'by cottys plut and her nayle' and another by the same oath, p. 150.

two rushes. Cp. *Narcissus* (ed. Lee), 488: 'here's no hunter woorth two rushes.'

795. *the Clerigalls.* Cp. l. 994 'the villaine hath byn in as many Clerigalls in his life as I have gathered phrases' and 1770 'who should make mee hold my [tongue] they? *P.* Not wee, but the Clericals shall.' Dr Murray in the

N.E.D. considers the word to be a corrupted form of 'clarichord' = 'clavichord,' a stringed musical instrument, and in its penal sense to mean a constable, 'perhaps because their whips were stringed instruments,' herein following Mr Macray, editor of the Parnassus Plays, and apparently only knowing the word as it occurs in the *Returne from Parnassus*, Pt. I. It there appears twice, first in IV. I. 1269, 'I bespoke you a pasport, least the clarigols att some town's ende catche you,' and again in V. 2. 1544, 'Let us loiter noe longer, leaste the clarigoles catche us.' But if the word in these two instances can bear the meaning 'constables,' it cannot do so in the second example, at any rate, of its use in the present play. The only meaning which seems to fit all cases is 'stocks.' And I believe that 'stocks' is what the word does mean. Cooper in his *Annals of Cambridge* (III. 22) quotes from the town-accounts under the year 1606 'Item, for a payre of Claricalls at Sturbridge fayre, ij*s*. iiij*d*.' Under 1564 (II. 208) Cooper quotes an entry 'Item, for ij lockes to hange upon the stocks ij*s*. viij*d*.' and under 1569 (II. 244) 'Item, for carrienge of the Pillorie to the faier & setting it up, vj*d*.'

810. *scuse*, excuse. Cp. the form 'fect,' l. 447.

813. *Jesus blesse me.* In Dekker's *Satiromastix*, Sir Vaughan uses the oath 'Jesu pless us.'

814. *such learned men, that conjure the devill into a circle and put him againe in hell.* Cp. l. 1831. For the popular association of learning with magic, cp. *Merry Devil of Edmonton* (Hazlitt-Dodsley, X. 257): 'I have heard of one that is a great magician, But he's about the university'; Jonson, *Every Man in his Humour*, IV. 4. 20: '*Know.* But how should he know thee to be my man? *Brai.* Nay, sir, I cannot tell; unless it be by the black art. Is not your son a scholar sir? *Know.* Yes, but I hope his soul is not allied Unto such hellish practice.'

815. *put [the devill] againe in hell.* This feat of sorcery is referred to in one of the most indecent stories of the *Decamerone* of Boccaccio.

818. *muske companions*, fashionable gentlemen scented with musk. Cp. Stubbes, *Anatomie of Abuses* (1585, reprint 1836), p. 73: 'Is not this a sweet pride, to haue ciuet, muske...and suche lyke, whereof the smell may bee felte and perceaued, not onely all ouer the house or place where they bee present, but also a stones cast off almost,—yea, the bed wherein they haue layd their delicate bodyes, the places where they haue sate, the clothes and thinges which they haue touched, shall smelle a weeke, a moneth, and more, after they be gone.' *Soliman and Perseda* (T. Hawkins, *Ancient Drama*, II. 213): '*Piston.* ...he wears civet And when it was ask'd him where he had that musk, He said, all his kindred smelt so.' Gascoigne, *Steele Glas*, Epilogus: 'They [women] marre with muske the balme which nature made'; *Returne from Parnassus*, Pt. I. 911: 'I had a muske jerkin layde all with golde lace'; Pt. II. 1406: 'one that dreams in a night of nothing but musk and civet';

Jonson, *Every Man out of his Humour*, II. I (Bang's *Materialien*, l. 1015): 'he sleepes with a musk-cat euery night, and walkes all day hang'd in pomander chaines.'

824. *cry quit with him*, be even with him. This is an earlier example of the phrase than those given in the *N.E.D.*

830. *I dare pawne my maidenhead.* Cp. l. 856. Cp. T. Cook, *The City Gallant* (Hazlitt-Dodsley, XI. 203): '*Joyce.* By my maidenhead, an oath which I ne'er took in vain'; *Wily Beguil'd* (Hazlitt-Dodsley, IX. 303): '*Peg.* I durst ha' sworn by my maidenhead (God forgive me that I should take such an oath)'.

831. *cut queane me* (cp. l. 854 *cuckqueand*), make a cutquean, cuckquean or female cuckold of me. The *N.E.D.* (which entirely dissociates 'cuck-quean' from 'cot-quean,' 'a housewife, a scold') quotes for the verb Warner, *Alb. Eng.* (1592), VIII. 41 (1612), 199: 'Came I from France to be cuck-quean'd here?'

838. *brownest*, ugliest. The use seems not recognized in the *N.E.D.* Cp. the first words of a 'jig' quoted in a note in *Old English Plays* (1815), VI. 331: 'Did you not say to me before That I was a jade and a common whore? And swore that you would knock me down Because I ugly was and brown?'

844. *as far in*, 'as much in my intimacy' (in a double sense). The *N.E.D.* only recognizes this use when 'with' follows as in Bunyan, *Holy War* (1682): 'they had been in with Diabolus.'

846. *in my taking*, in my case, in my state of mind. Cp. ll. 2200, 2354, 2799, and *Marriage of Wit and Science* (Hazlitt-Dodsley, II. 376): 'We shall leave the gentleman in a pretty taking'; *Two Angry Women of Abington* (*ibid.* VII. 306): 'He's in a fine taking'; (*ibid.* 351): 'I would not...anybody should see me in this taking.'

847. *deaven*, good even. Not in the *N.E.D.* Cp. however *Gammer Gurton's Needle*, IV. 2: 'God deven, dame Chat...God deven, my friend Diccon.'

858. *thats counsell*, that's a secret. See *N.E.D.*

880. *great*, very friendly to one another. Cp. J. Cook, *The City Gallant* (Hazlitt-Dodsley, XI. 231): 'time must shake good-fortune by the hand before you two must be great; 'specially you, sister' [with a *double entente*]; Chapman, *May Day*, I. I: 'Francischina, with whom I hear thou art ready to lie down, thou art so great with her. *Ang.* I am as great as a near kinsman may be with her, sir, not otherwise.'

884. *worke them*, work upon them. Cp. *Winter's Tale*, V. 3. 58: 'if I had thought the sight of my poor image would thus have wrought you.'

885. *give them the unset*, give them the onset, make a start with them, accost them. Cp. *Marriage of Wit and Science* (Hazlitt-Dodsley, II. p. 366): 'This is the deadly den, as far as I perceive, Approach we near, and valiantly let us the onset give.'

889. *doe you thinke that there are beares at our house?* Cp. l. 1137 *n.*

928. *gill*, wench, lass (used contemptuously). Cp. Preston, *Cambises*, *ad fin.*: '*King* (to Queen). Thou cursed jil.'

946. *a Cudgill play.* The *N.E.D.* has no earlier quotation than T. Randall, *in Ann. Dubrensia* (1636, ed. 1877), p. 19: 'What is the Barriers but a Courtly way Of our more downe-right sport the Cudgell-play?'

961. *Gods bodikens.* Cp. Shakspeare, *Merry Wives*, II. 3. 46: 'Body-kins'; *Hamlet*, II. 2. 554: 'Gods bodykins.'

972. *passe.* The word apparently means 'pass or exceed the mark,' so as to become liable to censure. I know no exact parallel. In *Timon of Athens*, I. I. 12 ('he passes') the word is applied to *merit* transcending expectation.

983. *kennell thoughts.* 'Kennel' means the gutter or channel in the street which received unclean refuse. The *N.E.D.* quotes a similar use of 'kennel' as an adjective='low, coarse,' from E. Gilpin, *Skial.* (1598, ed. 1878), 5: 'That men should haue such kennel wits.'

991. *fitted*, punished. The *N.E.D.* quotes Fletcher, *Hum. Lieutenant* (before 1625), IV. I: 'If I do not fit ye let me frie for it.'

992. *last*, laced, beaten. Cp. l. 1244, 'sweete fast'='sweetfaced.' Cp. *Two Angry Women of Abington* (1599) (Hazlitt-Dodsley, VII. 359): 'Now my back hath room to reach: I do not love to be lac'd in, when I go to lace a rascal.'

995. *gathered phrases.* The culling of phrases from good authors was an important part of the work of a young student of rhetoric at school or at the University. Cp. *Pedantius* (Bang's *Materialien*, l. 1484, etc.): 'Ciceronianissimum puerum!...vides tu jam quid sit ex Epistolis Tullij familiaribus colligere phrases plusquam familiares?'

996. *I must be the man that must make the Clownes yeald when all is done.* Cp. *Wily Beguil'd* (1606) (Hazlitt-Dodsley, IX. 275): '*Churms.* I see that Churms must be the man must carry Lelia, when all's done.'

1003. *greasie*, filthy. Cp. Marston, *Scourge of Villainie* (1598), I. 3. 79: 'greasie Aretine.'

1021. *if I be not on your skirts.* Mr McKerrow gives me the following illustrations of this phrase: Puttenham, *Arte of English Poesie*, ed. Haslewood, 1811, pp. 252—3: 'to speake faire to a mans face, and foule behinde his backe, to set him at his trencher and yet sit on his skirts for so we vse to say by a fayned friend'; Bernard's *Terence*, ed. 1607, p. 66, *Andria*, III. v. (last line): '*Te vlciscar*, I will be reuenged on thee: I will sit on thy skirts: I will be vpon your iacke for it.'

1023. *putt into the blacke bill.* 'Black bill,' as Mr McKerrow suggests, is probably equivalent to 'black book,' *i.e.* 'a book recording the names of persons who have rendered themselves liable to censure or punishment'

(*N.E.D.*). Such a book seems to have been kept at the Universities by the Proctors. Cp. Spenser, *Sonn.* X.: 'All her faults in thy black booke enroll.'

1026. *a company of good* [*fellows*]. Cp. l. 1186.

1032. *adjuvants*, helpers, assistants. The first quotation for the word as a subs. in the *N.E.D.* is of the date 1609, viz. Yelverton in *Archæ.* XV. 51 (T): 'I have only been a careful Adjuvant, and was sorry I could not be the efficient.'

1036. *Collierly.* See l. 222 *n.*

1037. *stand here...like John Drome*, *i.e.* like one turned out of a house. The phrase 'Jack, John, or Tom Drum's entertainment' denoted, says the *N.E.D.*, 'a rough reception, turning an unwelcome guest out of doors.' It quotes Gosson, *School of Abuse* (1579): 'Plato...gaue them...Drummes entertainment, not suffering them once to shew their faces in a reformed common wealth'; and J. Taylor, in *Coryats Crudities* (1613): 'Not like the entertainment of Iacke Drum Who was best welcome when he went his way.'

1066. *crackropes*, rogues. Similar formations are 'waghalter,' 'crackhalter.'

1067. *take her heels.* Cp. l. 1351. Mr McKerrow points out that the common phrase at this date was 'take his heels,' not 'take to his heels.' Thus we have in Puttenham, *Arte of English Poesie*, ed. Haslewood (1811), p. 229: 'if an Historiographer shal write of an Emperor...how...hee ioyned battel...and...ranne out of the fielde, and tooke his heeles.'

1071. *shrodly*, shrewdly, exceedingly. Cp. Chettle and Day, *The Blind Beggar of Bednall Green* (Bang's *Materialien*), l. 1887: 'Hee's shrowdly frighted.'

1086. *muttonmonger*, lascivious person, whoremaster. Cp. Chapman, *May Day*, II.: 'as if you were the only noted mutton-monger in all the city. *Lor.* Well, Angelo, heaven forgive us the sins of our youth'; III. 'there shall the old flesh-monger fast for his iniquity.'

1118. *whatsomever we do.* Whitney, *Century Dictionary*, quotes from the *Babees Book* (E.E.T.S.), p. 45: 'whatsumeuere thee betide.'

1126. *Boggards*, privies.

1129. *my marke*, the object I am about to attack. Cp. Shaks. *Sonnet* 70. 2: 'slander's mark was ever yet the fair.'

logerpate, loggerhead. The word is not in the *N.E.D.*

1137. *blinde Bayard*, a phrase constantly used to denote blind recklessness. The reference is to Bayard, the magic steed given by Charlemagne to Rinaldo. Cp. *Proverbs* of J. Heywood, ed. Sharman, p. 33: 'who so bold as blinde Bayard is?'

heres a beare will bite you. Mr McKerrow suggests that there may be an allusion to the phrase 'Good bear, bite not' used to an angry person. Cp. Nashe, *Strange Newes*, H 3 (*Wks.* (ed. McKerrow), I. 307. 8—10): 'Euerie milke-maide can gird with, Ist true? How saie you, lo? who would haue thought it? Good Beare, bite not. A man is a man though hee hath but a hose on his head'; Harvey, *Wks.* ed. Grosart, II. 244, and Nashe, III. 125. 31; 126. 5—6.

1144. *vild*, common Elizabethan form of 'vile.'

1147. *I marvell which of them could have invented such a thing.* A similar self-complacent attitude towards the abilities of University men is seen in the remark of the tailor in *Returne from Parnassus*, Pt. I. 495: 'if they had our wisdome joyned to their learninge they woulde prove grave men'; and that of Gullio, *ibid.* 1148: 'What man soever loves a crane The same he thinkes to be Diane. A dull universitie's head would have bene a month aboute thus muche!'

1153. *house of office*, perhaps here 'privy.' Cp. Chapman, *May Day*, IV.: 'my wife's coal-house and her other house of office annex'd to it.'

backsides, rear part of the buildings.

1158. *corner capp slaves.* The square cap worn by divines and members of the Universities was constantly called a 'corner cap.' Cp. Gascoigne, *Supposes*, V. 4: 'we will teach master doctor to wear a corner'd cap of a new fashion'; Stow, *Annals* (1605), 1432: 'The heads of the University of Cambridge all clad in Scarlet gownes and corner Caps'; *New Custom* (Hazlitt-Dodsley, III. 11): 'He will have priests no corner-cap to wear, surplices are superstition.'

1161. *what a wondring keepes thou at him.* Cp. Chaucer, *Squires Tale*, 300: 'ne was ther swich a wondring as was tho.'

1180. *fort*, 'for 't,' 'for it.' If this is the meaning however, 'for this' which follows becomes tautological.

1230. *a tricke...as shall cost you the setting on.* The meaning is not very clear. Cp. 1295 *n.*

1244. *sweete fast*, sweet faced. See l. 992 *n.*

1259. *pepper them*, punish them severely. Cp. *Romeo and Jul.* III. I. 102.

1260. *good*, my good man. Cp. Shaks. *Tempest*, I. I. 16: 'nay, good, be patient.'

1272. *right downe* (adj.). Cp. 'downe right' in l. 946 *n.*

1274. *doeing his endevour.* Cp. Robinson, *trans. of Utopia* (1551), I.: 'Doynge my endeuoure to....'

1295. *sett you in with a powder* (cp. l. 2149, *sett her out with a pox*). 'Set' seems to be used in these phrases in the sense 'put,' 'thrust.' I have not met with any parallel uses of 'set in,' 'set out.' 'With a powder' like 'with a pox' is an asseveration (='with a vengeance'). A powder was used to cure the pox, and so had an unpleasant association attached to it. The phrase is used in a punning sense in Shirley, *Traitor*, III. I: 'he hath...walked up and down...with a case of pistols charged, wherewith, as he partly confessed, he intended to send the duke to Heaven with a powder!'

1320. *thou didst performe thy office.* This is the explanation of his conduct which Niphle has resolved on. He has recourse to it at l. 1522.

1335. *let her pip pap* (cp. l. 1431, *to keepe pip pap in her house*). The sense is clear, though the expression is not given in the *N.E.D.* Cp. 'knicke knocke,' l. 1767, and 'tick tack' in *Lusty Juventus* (to a whore): 'You will to ticke tacke, I fere, If you had time'; in Lyly's *Mother Bombie*, V. 3 (in the Song): 'Such tick-tack has held many a day,...Then let them alone, they know what to do'; and in *Measure for Measure*, I. 2. 196.

1338. *tell her a tale of a tubb.* Cp. l. 1521 and J. Heywood's *Proverbs* (1546), ed. Sharman, p. 160; *Marriage of Wit and Science* (Hazlitt-Dodsley, II. 335): 'What should I make a broad tree of every little shrub, And keep her a great while with a tale of a tub?'; *Misogonus*, III. 2. 50 (in *Quellen und Forschungen*, LXXX.): 'I hope its but a tale of a tubb'; J. Clarke, *Paræmiologia* (1639), p. 8: 'You tell us a tale of a Tub. Sine capite fabula.'

1339. *trow*, 'I should like to ask.' Cp. *Cymbeline*, I. 6. 47: 'What is the matter, trow?'

1350. *puff shirken.* A buff jerkin was worn by fighting-men. Cp. N. Field, *A Woman is a Weathercock* (1612) (Hazlitt-Dodsley, XI. 60): 'What art?—A soldier; one that lives upon this buff jerkin,' and Dekker, *Satiromastix*, I. 2: 'scurvy limping-tongued captain, poor greasy buff-jerkin.'

1368. *I am for theise...Athenians.* Cp. l. 148 *n.*

1370. *nimbd*, took, filched. The first example in the *Century Dictionary* for this form of the pt. tense is Butler, *Hudibras*, I. 1. 598: 'nimm'd a cloak.'

the fineliest, in the finest manner. This form of the superl. adverb is not given in the *N.E.D.* Cp. l. 159 'the dayntelest.'

1377. *studies*, endeavours, aims. Cp. Shaks. *As you like it*, V. 2. 85: 'it is my study To seem...ungentle to you.'

1381. *hoisting of a clowne*, punishing (?). *Hoist* seems to mean properly 'to lift on the back to receive a flogging.'

1382. *looby*, lout, clown.

1422. *the search*, the search-party. Cp. Hazlitt-Dodsley, VII. 433.

1426. *Catts plood*, God's blood.

1428. *burst ope.* Cp. Shaks. *King John*, II. 1. 449: 'The mouth of passage shall we fling wide ope.'

1449. *kept my selfe with the good man.* Cp. B. Jonson, *Volpone*, II. 5: 'Get you a cittern, lady vanity, And be a dealer with the virtuous man'; and the maxim 'Cum bonis ambula' prefixed to Cato's *Distycha* (Lond. 1572) and ascribed in Fraunce's *Victoria*, l. 2154, to Periander.

1486. *credite...cract*, *i.e.* impaired, destroyed. Cp. W. Rowley, *A Woman never vext*, III.: '*Old Fost.* Undone for ever! my credit I have crack'd To buy a venture, which the sea has soak'd.'

1497. *Chopper...Lockwood.* Cricket pretends to be setting dogs on the pursuit. The name 'Rocwood' is given to a dog in *Lingua*, V. 17.

1498. *lyes out.* I can find no instance of this phrase in the *N.E.D.* or elsewhere. It apparently means 'holds aloof from the chase.'

villonestly, villainously. Cp. the vulgar pronunciation 'nice-tly' for 'nicely.'

1499. *trayled him out*, got on his trail and drove him out. Cp. Shaks. *Hamlet* IV. 5. 109: 'How cheerfully on the false trail they cry!'

1500. *a start, a start.* Apparently the cry of onlookers when the hunted animal breaks covert. Perhaps in Shaks. *Henry V.* III. I. 23: 'like greyhounds in the slips, straining upon the start,' 'the start' means also the breaking away of the hare. Cp. *I. Henry IV.* I. 3. 198: 'to start a hare'; and *Twelfth Night*, IV. I. 63: 'he started one poor heart [play on "hart"] of mine in thee.'

1523. *executing my office.* See l. 1320 and *Introduction*, p. xliii.

1531. *a two peny queane.* Cp. E. Sharpham, *The Fleire* (1607), 10 *recto*: 'they [*i.e.* "mercenarie women"] (like your common Players) let men come in for twopence a peece, and yet themselves to haue but the tenth penny.'

1558. *a garnish.* By a 'garnish' is meant 'money extorted from a new prisoner, either as a jailer's fee, or as drink-money for the other prisoners.' The *N.E.D.* quotes Greene, *Upstart Courtier* (1592), D. ii. a: 'Let a poore man be arrested...he shall be almost at an angels charge what with garnish...,' and Gay, *Beggar's Opera*, II. 7: '*Gaoler to a prisoner*: You know the custom sir. Garnish, Captain, Garnish.' Mr McKerrow refers me also to Dekker's *Seven Deadly Sins* (*Wks.* ed. Grosart, II. 46). It was provided by article 13 of the Composition between the University and the town in 1503 (Cooper's *Annals*, I. 266) that in the case of prisoners committed by the Chancellor, Vice-Chancellor, or their 'Lefetenante'—'the Keper of the said Prisons shall not take eny fees of eny Scoller etc....& of all other persons so comytted to prison by the Chancellor etc. the Keper of the said Prison shall have of eny suche other Person, for the first daie iiij*d.*, and yf he tarry there by one weke or longer, xij*d.*, & no more.' So a groat was the 'garnish' duly appointed.

1591. *least you should be proud of this great Triumph, after the ancient manner, you shall have this poor servant to be carried with you, that you may be humbled at the sight of her.* In a Roman triumph, in the same chariot with the victorious general rode a public slave, holding a crown over the general's head, and saying at intervals 'Look behind thee, remember that thou art a man.' Cp. Juvenal, *Sat.* X. 41: 'sibi consul Ne placeat, curru servus portatur eodem'; and Mayor's note on the passage.

1621. *the proudest of them all.* Cp. ll. 1726, 1775. A popular expression in such a connexion. Cp. *Respublica*, V. 8. 35 (*Quellen und Forschungen*, LXXX.): 'Not the prowdest of them all can hurte me with a heare.'

1624. *buske point*, 'the lace with its tag which secured the end of the busk' (Nares, quoted by the *N.E.D.*). The busk was 'a strip of wood, whalebone, steel, etc. passed down the front of a corset to strengthen it.' The first quotation given in the *N.E.D.* is from Marston, *Scourge of V.* (1599): 'I saw him court his mistresse looking-glasse, worship a busk-point.'

1637. *your shinns burne.* I have not traced this phrase. Does it mean 'you have a guilty conscience of that'? Or is it a reference to a particular symptom of a certain disease?

1639—41. Luce here reminds one of Carmen in Mérimée's wonderful story.

1646. *battbond.* This form is not given in the *N.E.D.*

1649. *thy tongue is no slander.* Probably Luce means 'slanderer,' as Dogberry in *Much Ado*, V. 1. 221: 'they [these men] are slanders.'

1658. *ruffle in Rhetorke*, bluster, swagger, or 'show off' in rhetoric. Cp. *Wily Beguil'd* (T. Hawkins, *Ancient Drama*, III. 342): '*Nurse.* He does so ruffle before my mistress with his barbarian eloquence, and strut before her in a pair of Polonian legs.' If 'Rhetorke' is not a mere scribe's error, we may parallel it by a similar distortion in R. W.'s *Three Ladies of London* (Hazlitt-Dodsley, VI. 267): 'Thou art...full of thy rope-ripe—I would say rethoric.'

1662. *Orlando furioso.* R. Greene's play *The Historie of Orlando Furioso*, played as early as 159½, was printed in 1594 and again in 1599.

1663. *Layis.* No play called *Lais* seems to be known. Lais is a character in Gnapheus' *Acolastus*, which was translated by Palsgrave in 1540. A play 'Acolastus,' probably Gnapheus' Latin original, was acted at Trinity College, Cambridge, in 1560.

1687. *torchbearer to the Devil.* 'Plays' perhaps suggest 'torchbearer' because masquers were ushered in by torchbearers.

1698. *your stomacke*, your pride.

1705. *being in so good doeinges*, leading such a good life.

1708. *what rules next?* Luce's varying moods are thought of as planets ruling men's actions in turn. Cp. *II. Henry VI.* IV. 4. 16: 'hath this lovely face Ruled, like a wandering planet, over me?'

1720. (*quickned*) *with a ffoxe taile, will you not?* The *N.E.D.* says that a foxtail was formerly one of the badges of the fool or jester, and that the phrase 'a flap with a foxtail' appears to mean 'a contemptuous dismissal.' Perhaps Luce means, 'Instead of whipping me, you will let me go easily, won't you?' She then plays on the phrase in another sense. Cp. *Kyng Daryus* (*Quellen und Forschungen*, LXXX. 367): '*Iniquytie.* Hee dyd here so on me rayle. But I thynke, I gaue him a blowe with a foxe tayle. So he was gone quycly from mee, He durst tarye no longer in my companie. *Importunytie.* Thou didest serue him well'; 370: 'We will hym in our snares trappe And hym with a Foxtayle wee wyll flappe.'

1723. *quicke*, with child. Cp. Middleton and Rowley, *The Spanish*

Gipsy, IV.: '*Car.* 'cause you are in haste, I am quick; I am a maid—— *John* (*aside*). So! so! a maid quick?'

1729. *Captaine Carifeild.* This may possibly be Ralph Garfeild citizen of London and a member of the Dyers' Company or his son Benjamin Garfeild. Ralph Garfeild's will was made in 1607. In it he speaks of his interest in two ships 'The *Fawlcon* of Ipswich' and the '*Rose* of Ipswich.' When the will was proved 2 Nov. 1608, his son Benjamin was in parts beyond the sea. Another son, Abraham Garfeild, was of Catharine Hall, Cambridge. See W. P. W. Phillimore, *The Garfield Family in England*, Boston, 1883.

1730. *the worst lucke myne.* One would expect 'the *worse*,' etc. Cp. Milton, *Areopagitica*, *ad in.*: 'natural endowments haply not the worst for two and fifty degrees of northern latitude.'

this 3. *yeares daye*, since this day three years ago. Cp. *Impacyente pouerte* (pr. 1560), ll. 865—866: 'Alas my men are from me clene I se them not this seuen nyghtes daye'; *II. Henry VI.* II. I. 2: 'I saw not better sport these [=this] seven years' day.' The *N.E.D.* quotes Tindal (1526), *Acts* X. 30: 'this daye nowe iiij dayes I fasted'; but gives no example of the phrase with the qualifying words preceding 'day.'

1759. *Kisse Mr Nifle behind.* Cp. J. Heywood, *Play of the Wether* (*Quellen und Forschungen*, LXXX. 243): '*M.* I neuer desyred to kys you before. *L.* Why haue ye alway kyst her behynde?'

1764. *Camero.* The sense is plain, but the word is not in the *N.E.D.* 'Camarero' in Spanish is a valet, and 'camarera' a waiting-maid.

punck, courtesan.

1767. *knicke knocke.* The word in the sense in which it seems to be used here is not found in the *N.E.D.* See l. 1335 *n.*

1775. *looke through a hemping windowe.* This humorous phrase for 'be hanged' is not given in the *N.E.D.*, which however gives a similar one from Nashe, *Unfort. Trav.* (1594): 'I...scapde dauncing in a hempen circle.' For the form 'hemping' for 'hempen,' cp. Phaer, *Æneid*, V. 552 (1558): 'the hemping corde.'

1783. *thou plaiest thy prises.* 'To play prizes, to fight publicly for a prize; hence figuratively, to contend only for show' (*Century Dictionary*). Cp. J. Cook, *The City Gallant* (Hazlitt-Dodsley, XI. 249): 'Now dost thou play thy prize;...if you can do any good...the silver game be yours'; and Stillingfleet (quoted in the *Century Dictionary*): 'By their endless disputes and wranglings about words and terms of art, they [the philosophers] made the people suspect they did but play prizes before them.'

1799. *dismounting.* Cp. l. 1875. The *N.E.D.* gives *dismount*, 'to degrade, depose,' and quotes one example of 1651, and N. Bacon, *Disc. Govt. Eng.* II. XIII. (1739), 69: 'Dukes were dismounted without conviction.'

1807. *billie Colbie.* Colby represents as I believe (see *Introduction*, p. xlvii)

William Nicholson. Probably however 'billie' here is the Northern word (='fellow,' 'friend').

putt it up, put up with it. Cp. *Returne from Parnassus*, Pt. I. 633: 'can a man be galde by povertie...and put it up like a Stoick?'

1808. *goe out prison.* Cp. l. 2804: 'make her shurney out towne'; and Shaks. *Coriol.* V. 2. 41: 'pushed out your gates the very defender of them.'

1810. *thwake their Jackes*, belabour their jackets or jerkins. Cp. ll. 1834 and 1021 *n.* Cp. N. Field, *Amends for Ladies* (1618) (Hazlitt-Dodsley, XI. 138): 'they are...cowards...If I thought so, I would be upon the jack of one of them instantly.'

1811. *strammell*, lanky, overgrown (?). Cp. *The English Dialect Dictionary*: '*Strammel* (Shropshire). A lean, gaunt, illfavoured person or animal. "What a great strammel of a pig that is as John bought!"' Possibly we have the same word in Jonson, *Every Man out of his Humour*, V. 5. 3761: 'fed with it, the whorson strummell patcht goggle-ey'd Grumbledories would ha' Gigantomachized.'

1826. *Jackes*, contemptible fellows.

1828. *scrubbes*, drudges.

perke, pert, uppish. Cp. Spenser, *Shepheards Calendar*, February, 8: 'perke as a peacock.'

1829. *take them downe a hole lower.* Cp. Lyly, *Endymion* (1591), III. 3: '*Epi.* He hath taken his thoughts a hole lower'; and Shirley, *Triumph of Peace*: '*Tai.* Knock down my wife!...I'll bring him a button hole lower.'

1830. *the slaves will crowe over us.* Cp. l. 2173. The *N.E.D.* quotes J. Udall, *Demonst. Discip.*: 'They crow ouer them as if they wer their slaues.'

1831. *they are seene in the blacke art, they will make us all daunce naked.* Cp. l. 814. Cp. Marlowe, *Faustus*, Sc. VIII. (IX.): '*Robin.* I ha' stolen one of Doctor Faustus' conjuring books...Now will I make all the maidens in our parish dance at my pleasure stark naked before me.' Reginald Scot in *The Discouerie of Witchcraft*, Bk. XIII. Ch. XXX. shows how this supposed achievement of magic can be simulated by jugglery: 'To make one danse naked. Make a poore boie confederate with you. so as after charmes etc. spoken by you, he uncloth himselfe, and stand naked, seeming (whilest he undresseth him) to shake, stampe and crie, still hastening to be unclothed, till he be starke naked: or if you can procure none to go so far, let him onelie beginne to stampe and shake etc., and to uncloth him, and then you may (for the reverence of the company) seeme to release him.'

1837. *lamb'd.* The *N.E.D.* quotes Thomas' *Dictionary* (1596): '*Defusto* to lamme or bumbast with strokes.' 'Belam' is found a year earlier.

1841. *waster play.* 'Waster' is defined in the *Century Dictionary* as 'a wooden sword formerly used for practice by the common people.' I am inclined to think however that here 'waster play' = 'cudgel-play.' Cp. l. 946 and Chettle and Day, *Blind Beggar of Bednall Green* (Bang's *Materialien*), 2460: 'I can play at wasters as well as another man; but all's one for that, give me but an ashen Gibbet in my hand...an ashen Plant, a good Cudgell.'

1843. *clapper clawe*, claw, beat. Cp. *Merry Wives*, III. 3. 67: 'He will clapper-claw thee tightly, bully.'

1847. *pay them backe and side.* Cp. *Narcissus* (ed. Lee), 426: 'I'll pay his breeche.'

backe and side. Cp. *Candlemas Day* (Hawkins, *Ancient Drama*, I. 7): 'They shall suffre woo and peyne thrugh bak and syde'; and *ibid. inf.*: '*Watkyn.* I shud bete you bak and side tyll it were blewe.'

1863. *Runt*, young ox, a boor or hoiden. Cp. Fletcher, *Wit without Money*, V. 2: 'Before I buy a bargain of such runts I'll buy a college for bears and live among 'em.' Mris Colbie is referring to Tavie.

1877—9. 'if only thy success answers to my expectations, we shall then have our enemies as humble suppliants for our favour.'

1884. *you come as just as Jermyns lippe* (*i.e.* very unpunctually). The phrase is not in the *N.E.D.* Cp. J. Heywood's *Proverbs*, ed. Sharman, p. 96: 'When birds shall roost, (quoth he), at viii, ix, or ten, Who shall appoynt their house, the cock or the hen? The hen, (quoth shee); the cocke, (quoth he); just, (quoth she), As Jermans lips.' The editor quotes from Latimer's *Remains*: 'As just as German's lips, which came not together by nine mile'—and from Gosson's *School of Abuse*: 'Agree like Dogge and Catte, and meete as just as Germans lippes.'—Mr McKerrow sends me the following additional examples. Harington, *An Apologie* (1596), Cc 2 *v.*: 'Rara auis in terris nigroque similimo [*sic*] Cigno; Iust as Iermins lippes, nowe you haue compared him well, as white as a black swan.' Dekker, *Batchelars Banquet* (*Wks.* ed. Grosart, i. 206), side note: 'Just as Iarmās lips.'

1911. *I goe to my witts to*, I set myself thinking how to.... Cp. Shaks. *Measure for Measure*, III. 1. 171: 'tomorrow you must die; go to your knees and make ready.'

1916. *an iniquitie*, a shameless character. A reference to the character of Iniquity or the Vice in the Morality Plays. Cp. *Richard III.* III. 1. 82: 'Like to the formal vice, Iniquity'; and *I. Henry IV.* II. 4. 449: 'that reverend vice, that grey iniquity' [applied to Falstaff].

1917. *flurtes*, women of giddy, flighty character (*N.E.D.*).

1934. *bills*, placards, notices. Cp. 'Articles against the Master of St John's College Dec. 1565' (*Eagle*, XXVIII. p. 150): 'whereas our Statutes dothe prescrybe...that the mastership after everie vacation should be vacante xij daies and that the president shoulde sette upp a bille of the vacation thereof.'

1948. *heigh Saint Tavie is a welsh man borne.* Is this a scrap of a song?

1951. *masse*, mace.

1952. *knowe her selfe*, know her place and realize her situation, limitations. Cp. *Macbeth*, IV. 2. 19: 'But cruel are the times when we are traitors, And do not know ourselves'; and II. 2. 73: '*Lady M*....Be not lost so poorly in your thoughts. *Macb*....To know my deed, 'twere best not know myself.' This use of the reflexive verb does not seem to be very clearly treated either by Schmidt or by the *N.E.D.*

1959. *discomininge.* The purport of the Rector's bills had been to prohibit members of the University under heavy penalties from having any dealings with some of the leaders of the town-party. Brecknocke being a chandler had suffered severely in pocket by the prohibition. For the University's power of discommoning, see *Introduction*, pp. xv, xvi.

1968. *prittle prattle.* Cp. T. Heywood, *Royal King and Loyal subject*, I.: '*Welshman*: Awe-man, you prittle and prattle nothing but leasings and untruths.'

1969. *ranke.* Cp. l. 242.

1970. *for cods.* Cp. l. 2248 *n.*

1976. *shitten knave.* Cp. *Gammer Gurton's Needle*, V. 2: 'Thou shitten knave.'

1995. *crush a pott...of Ale*, *i.e.* drink, quaff, 'discuss' it. The *N.E.D.* quotes Greene, *Def. Conny Cat.* (1592) (*Wks.* ed. Grosart, XI. 43): 'If euer I brought my Conny but to crush a potte of ale with mee'; and Shaks. *Romeo and Juliet*, I. 2. 86: 'come and crush a cup of wine.'

1996. *Ale...as good as ever was turne* [*? turned*] *over the tongue.* Cp. *Returne from Parnassus*, Pt. I. 584: 'I have as good a cupp of ale as ere was turnde over tonge, as they saye.'

1998. *game at Tables*, backgammon.

2001. *Methiglen.* Cp. l. 2806. Metheglin was a kind of mead made in Wales. Cp. Harrison's *Desc. of Eng.* in Holinshed (1587), p. 170 b: 'the Welshmen make no lesse accompt [of metheglin]...then the Greekes did of their Ambrosia or Nectar'; T. Heywood, *A Challenge for Beauty*, V. (song): 'The Brittaine he Metheglen quaffs, The Irish aqua-vitæ.' In B. Barnes, *Devil's Charter*, l. 1522 (and elsewhere) we have the curious soubriquet for the drink, 'mathew Glynne.' In E. Sharpham, *The Fleire*, III. *ad fin.*, a Welshman is named 'Maister Metheglins.'

2014. *wagpastie*, a term applied to a boy. Cp. *Jack Juggler* (Hazlitt-Dodsley, II. 141): 'this wage-pasty is either drunken or mad'; *Ralph Roister Doister*, III. 2 (*ibid.* III. 97): 'Maid, with whom are ye so hasty? *Tib.* Not with you, Sir, but with a little wage-pasty: A deceiver of folks by subtle craft and guile.' *Misogonus*, II. 4. 190. The sense of the word is not clear, especially as in two cases above it is spelt 'wage-pasty' (where 'wage-'

probably was taken to mean 'wager'). We have forms, however, which may be analogous in 'wag-string' (*Two Angry Women of Abington*, Hazlitt-Dodsley, VII. 279), 'wag-halter' and 'wagtail' (in which 'wag' has a transitive force) and 'wagmoire' (Spenser, *Sheph. Cal.* Sept. 130), a dialectic form of 'quagmire' or 'quake mire.' If 'wagpastie' is formed analogously to 'wagmoire' it may mean 'quivering pasty'—(one still calls a boy 'a piece of quicksilver'). If 'wag-' has a transitive force, the original meaning of the word is obscure. The word 'wag,' a merry fellow, is conjectured by Wedgwood to be short for 'waghalter.'

2020. *pie my traunt.* Cp. l. 632 *n.*

2029. *Its [no] madder for datt.* Cp. l. 643 *n.*

2030. *cuffer.* The *N.E.D.* has no example of the word before 1662.

2041. *heash.* Perhaps a misreading of 'Arsh' ('arse').

2049. *crosse*, across. The *N.E.D.* quotes an example of this aphetic form of the adverb from B. Googe (1586): 'cast bowes of Willowe crosse.'

2068. *while*, until.

2073. *till the shenerall behiett*, till the general give command. This is the best I can make of the reading of the MS. which suggests that the passage was not understood by the scribe. I take 'behiett' as = 'behight,' which is twice (incorrectly) used by Spenser in the sense 'command' (*F. Queene*, IV. 2. 39, and *Muiopotmos*, 241). One might also conjecture 'till the shenerall (the populace) be mett.'

2075. *bad utterance*, wrongful disposal. The *Century Dictionary* quotes Sandys, *Travailes*, p. 95: 'the English have so ill utterance (=bad sale) for their warm clothes in these hot countries,' and Hakluyt, *Voyages*, I. 300: 'what of our comodities haue most vtterance there.'

2076. *for my cause that the strange theeves did hericke from me in Lent.* I can make nothing of the word 'hericke.' Rumford is a butcher (cp. l. 2596) and the general reference is no doubt to the custom of prohibiting Cambridge butchers from selling flesh in Lent unless specially licensed by the Vice-Chancellor. It is not clear whether the word 'strange' means 'strange' or is meant for 'strang,' nor whether Rumford's grievance is against the University authorities directly, or against some butchers from outside Cambridge who, under the protection of the University, took his custom.

2087. *whist*, hushed, still.

2094. *play*, fence, play with cudgels or wasters.

2099. *hold*, bet, stake. A frequent use in the 16th century.

2114. *gamester like*, 'sportsmanlike.' No example of this sense in the *N.E.D.*

2125. *artificially*, skilfully.

2141. *take up against him*, take up the odds against (?). The compound verb has a personal object in Shaks. *II. Henry IV.* I. 3. 73: 'One power against the French, And one against Glendower; perforce a third must take us up.'

2144. *spoyle*, disturb, interrupt, as in *Lear*, V. 3. 278: 'these same crosses spoil me.'

2149. *sett her out with a pox.* See l. 1295 *n.*

2151. *gamesters*, players, fencers.

2163. *northen tieke*, northern cur. In its original sense 'tike' is found in *Lear*, III. 6. 73: 'bobtail tike or trundle-tail'; in its transferred sense in the *Pleasant Historie of Thomas of Reading* (Thoms' *Romances*, I. 102): 'the flirts and fromps which that Northerne tike gave me'; and in R. Anton, *Philosophers Satyrs* (1617), p. 65: 'The Northerne Tike is faire, grosse, dull and hard, The Southerne man more pliant.' For the form 'Northen,' cp. *Returne from Parnassus* (edition A of 1606), 392: 'the Northen winde' [where the existing MS. has 'Northern'].

2167. *drudger.* The first example of the word in the *N.E.D.* comes from Johnson's *Dictionary* (1755).

2170. *garre*, Northern English for 'make.' Cp. l. 2181 *n.*

2179. *must her tongue walke.* Cp. l. 2196. Cp. *Lingua*, II. 5 *ad fin.*: 'Madam, I pray you let your Pages tongue walk with us a little, till you return again'; Shirley, *Hyde Park*, II. 2: '*Bona.* I am a stranger. *Lacy.* Your tongue does walk our language.'

2181. *loape*, run. The word is again used in a passage of Northern dialect in Greene, *James IV.* Induction: 'This whinyard has gard many better men to lope then thou.'

2185. *Companions*, fellows.

2248. *under a stall.* Cp. l. 2285.

for gods. For this form of oath in which the substantive following the possessive is omitted, cp. l. 1970 and Beaumont and Fletcher, *Knight of the Burning Pestle*, I. 4 *ad fin.*: 'bid the players send Ralph, or by Gods—an they do not, I'll tear some of their perriwigs beside their heads.' Cp. also the commoner phrases 'By god's precious,' 'Sprecious,' 'O dear,' and the modern American 'O my.'

2250. *varte*, verity.

2254. *dry beaten*, soundly beaten. Cp. Chettle and Day, *Blind Beggar of Bednall Green* (Bang's *Materialien*), 2235: 'and I did not dry bang ye all one after another, I'de eat no meat but Mustard.' So l. 2461. *Pleasant Historie of Frier Rush* (Thoms' *Romances*, I. 298): 'with his forke he gatte him three or foure good dry stripes.'

2272. *Marcus Tullio Ricero*, Marcus Tullius Cicero. Mounsier's Latin is beyond correction.

2284. *hee gott and hidd himselfe.* The use of 'get and...' meaning 'go and...', 'set to work and...' is apparently not recognized in the *N.E.D.* Wright's *Dialect Dictionary* gives some examples, *e.g.* 'Git an' finish thee dinner.'

2294. *scirmige*, skirmish, 'scrimmage.' Cp. Peele, *Battle of Alcazar* (Malone Society), 1336: 'A long Skirmidge.'

2295. *lent me a fillip over the shoulders.* For this use of 'lent' the *N.E.D.* quotes Greene, *Art Coney Catch*, II.: 'The women...among whom he leant some lustie buffets.'

2296. *mett.* Cp. l. 146*n.*

2312. *Catches*, rounds. Cp. *Twelfth Night*, II. 3. 97.

2326. *laugh mee out of my clothes.* The phrase is not in the *N.E.D.*

2334. *Cogging*, cheating at dice.

2339. *under Butler.* Cp. l. 2833.

2345. *whiniard*, a Northern English term for 'sword.' Cp. l. 2181 *n.*

2346. *lurdains*, lubbers. Cp. l. 2487.

2353. *to a gray groat.* Cp. l. 2520. Cp. Chettle and Day, *Blind Beggar of Bednall Green* (Bang's *Materialien*), 1748: 'I have spent many a gray groat of honest swaggerers...and now I'll turn swaggerer my self'; *Misogonus* (*Quellen und Forschungen*, LXXX.), II. 4. 202: 'Ile not leave, bith fyue woundes, while I am worth a gree groat.' On this passage Brandl has a note, '(de) gree groat = Preisgroschen.' It seems more probable that the phrase is rightly written 'a grey groat' and means 'a silver groat.' Cp. *Respublica* (*ibid.*), V. 7. 24 (in dialect): 'a zilver grote.' It is not noticed in the *N.E.D.*

2356. *ganbelly.* I suppose this is a mistake for 'gorbelly,' which is defined in the *N.E.D.* 'a protuberant belly, or a person with such.'

2361. *Cranckling.* One would expect the sense 'jingling,' but the only meaning assigned to 'crankle' in the *N.E.D.* is 'bend in and out,' 'zigzag.'

2362. *make hast as fine as thou canst.* The *N.E.D.* illustrates the use of 'fine' as an adverb from Harding, *Chron.* C. V. (*c.* 1470): 'Ruling... full fine.'

2366. *shone*, shoes.

bound. In the original sense, 'ready for a journey.'

2375. *bald*, bawled.

2421. *emptie our Cofers in our Chambers.* It is clear that Cambridge tradesmen did not put their money in a bank. Cp. Shirley, *Witty Fair One* (1633), III. 5: '*Bra.* Oh, that I were a youth of one and twenty again...and ten thousand pounds in a musty coffer.'

2430. *Chist*, chest. Cp. Hall, *Virgidemiarum*, IV. 1. 21, 22: 'when his gout-swolne fist Gropes for his double ducates in his chist.'

2464. *a teephe Asse.* Is 'teephe' a corruption of 'tuphe' (toughe) = 'stubborn'? Or is it = 'hee-haw'? The whinny of a colt is represented by 'We-he-he' in *Trial of Treasure* (Hazlitt-Dodsley, III. 278).

2473. *tote*, to it.

2487. *wake*, quake. This northern form is appropriately given to

Rumford. The *N.E.D.* quotes the *Towneley Mysteries* (*c.* 1460): 'Euery man shall whake and gryse.'

2490. *hold it out*, keep it up. Cp. Shaks. *Merry Wives*, IV. 2. 141: 'Well said, brazen-face! hold it out.'

2503. *Alter mee no alters.* Cp. *Two Angry Women of Abington* (Hazlitt-Dodsley, VII. 285): 'hear me no hears'; etc., etc.

2508. *the spoile of us*, the ruin of us.

2524. *motions*, proposals.

2527. *backe that backe will.* Cp. *Respublica* (1553), I. 3. 18 (*Quellen und Forschungen*, LXXX.): 'catche that catche maye.'

2540. *Caponer.* Cp. l. 2562. Perhaps, in a passive sense, 'an unsexed coward.' The *N.E.D.* does not give the word, but quotes *capon*, to castrate, from Massinger, *Renegado* (1624), I. I: 'Had it been discovered, I had been caponed.'

2588. *horse and man.* Cp. Day, *Law Tricks*, IV. I: 'I am undone, horse and foot.'

2597. *in books.* Perhaps we should read 'in [my] books,' *i.e.* in my debt. Cp. *Returne from Parnassus*, Pt. I. 519: '*Draper*: as for those neat youths they are out of my books [*i.e.* in no favour with me]; and yet I lie, for they are more in them than the[y]'le pay in haste.'

2610. *I will not be offencible to you all.* Perhaps, 'I will not expose myself to the attacks of you all.' One might expect, 'I will not expose myself to be attacked by the University on behalf of you all,' but it is not easy to get this meaning out of the words. The *N.E.D.*, which defines the word as 'hurtful,' 'offensive,' quotes Hellowes, *Guevara Fam. Ep.* (1574): 'any enterprise that naturaly is seditious or offensible.'

2630. *upon thyne owne head*, unsolicited (= Latin *ultro*). The *N.E.D.* quotes Tomson, *Calvin's Serm. Tim.* (1579): 'That he (S. Paul) thrust not in himselfe, vppon his owne head, but that he was appointed of God.'

2655. *weele fitt them for a paire of*—[Clerigals?].

2666. *proper meetings.* 'Proper' is used ironically.

2670. *carried your mothers Tallies after her.* Cp. W. Rowley, *A Woman never Vext* (1632) (Hazlitt-Dodsley, XII. 138): '*Lambskin.* I have carried the tallies at my girdle seven years together' [? when he was an apprentice]. Tallies were sticks on which notches were cut to keep accounts by.

2681. *makes a legg.* The *N.E.D.* defines 'a leg' as 'an obeisance made by drawing back one leg and bending the other, a bow, scrape.' Cp. *Triumphs of Love and Fortune* (1589) (Hazlitt-Dodsley, VI. 177): 'When I come to a rich man's gate, I make a low leg, and then I knock there'; *Returne from Parnassus*, Pt. II. 963: 'let mee define a meere Scholler...He is one that cannot make a good legge.'

2686. *hot spurd*, fiery, impetuous. The adj. is used by Nashe in his *Unfortunate Traveller* (1594).

2688. *deele ha my saul.* Cp. *Ram Alley* (1611), V. (Hazlitt-Dodsley, X. 373): '*Oliver.* The devil take my soul, but I did love her. *Taf.* That oath doth show you are a Northern knight And of all men alive, I'll never trust A northern man in love. *Oliver.* And why? *Taf.* Because the first word he speaks is, the devil Take his soul....'

2713. *some warrs have passed you and us.* Perhaps 'passed'='befallen,' or we should read '*between* you and us.'

2715. *from*, apart from.

2716. *it was but superioritie, for which wee doe contend.* Cp. *Lingua*, II. 1: 'they [the Senses] fight for...a thing called Superiority, of which the Crown is but an Embleme.'

2731. *surquedrye*, over-confidence, arrogance. Cp. Chaucer, *Persones Tale*, 402: 'Presumpcion, is whan a man undertaketh an empryse, that him oghte nat do, or elles that he may nat do; and that is called Surquidrie'; *Pilgrim. to Parnassus*, 486: 'in Venus' surque[d]rie.' (Mr Macray strangely explains 'surquerie' as *suquerie*, 'sugariness.') Marston, *Ant. and Mel.* II. 3. 2.

2738. *being in their greatest triumph, when to us they are most serviceable*, who have no greater cause for pride than when, etc.

2741. *headbands*, fillets.

2749. *Take him downe*, humble him. Cp. *Romeo and Juliet*, II. 4. 159: 'an a' speak any thing against me, I'll take him down.'

2757. *three of his ofspringe*, perhaps Apollo, Diana and Minerva.

2758. *Monarchs...happy in philosophers familiarity*, *e.g.* Dionysius with Plato, Alexander with Aristotle.

2783. *to perfect our obedience*, to finish the task enjoined upon us by the Rector.

2798. *vas none take her up*, will no one take me into his service? Cp. *II. Henry IV.* II. 1. 199: 'you are to take soldiers up in counties.'

2806. *fitteling*, victualling.

2812. *entertaine*, take into service. Cp. Shirley, *Witty Fair One* (1633), II. 2: '*Treed.* Vouchsafe to entertain a servant, that shall study to command... his extremest possibilities in your business.'

2828. *make her shamber, vipe her bed, sweepe her shoes.* Tavie means, 'sweep your chamber, make your bed, wipe your shoes.'

2830. *of thy making*, of thy shape or kind. Cp. *Midsummer Night's Dream*, II. 1. 32: 'Either I mistake your shape and making quite.'

2833. *under skinker in the Buttery.* Prince Hal describes an underskinker in *I. Henry IV.* II. 4. 26.

2846. In the *Introduction*, p. liv, I expressed my doubt of the truth of Fuller's statement that townspeople were present at the original performance of *Club Law.* It will be noticed that the Epilogue is addressed solely and pointedly to members of the University, and gives no hint that other persons were included in the audience.

2850. *hobbenoles*, clowns, boors. The word is derived from Spenser's Hobbinoll in the *Shepheards Calendar*. The earliest example in the *N.E.D.* is from Heywood's *Love's Mistris* (1638), II.: 'This hobinall, this rusticke, this base clowne.'

2858. *attonment*, reconciliation.

2865. *Turne Herodotus, and one of his* 9. *Muses*, *i.e.* one of the books of his History, named severally after the Muses. Cp. *Lingua*, II. 1: '*Mend.* I helped Herodotus to pen some part of his Muses.'

INDEX OF WORDS AND PHRASES.

(Where the number of the line is printed in thick type, the expression is commented on in the Notes.)

CAMBRIDGE: PRINTED BY JOHN CLAY, M.A. AT THE UNIVERSITY PRESS.

Lightning Source UK Ltd.
Milton Keynes UK
01 December 2010

163669UK00001B/82/P